A New Treasury of
Children's Poetry

Selected and Introduced by
JOANNA COLE
Illustrated by Judith Gwyn Brown

A New Treasury of Children's Poetry

OLD FAVORITES AND NEW DISCOVERIES

DOUBLEDAY & COMPANY, INC.
GARDEN CITY, NEW YORK

Library of Congress Cataloging in Publication Data
Main entry under title:
A New treasury of children's poetry.
    Includes index.
    Summary: An anthology of more than 200 old and new poems for
preschool through adolescent readers.
    1. Children's poetry, American. 2. Children's poetry, English.
[1. American poetry — Collections. 2. English poetry — Collections]
I. Cole, Joanna. II. Brown, Judith Gwyn, ill.
PS586.3.N48 1984   811'.008'09282 82 20821
ISBN 0-385-18539-1

Grateful acknowledgment is made to the following for permission to reprint their copyrighted material. Every reasonable effort has been made to trace the ownership of all copyrighted poems included in this volume. Any errors which may have occurred are inadvertent and will be corrected in subsequent editions provided notification is sent to the publisher.

Bernice Wells Carlson. "The Puppy and the Kitty Cat" from *Listen and Help Tell the Story* by Bernice Wells Carlson. Copyright © 1965 by Abingdon Press. Used by permission. • *N. M. Bodecker.* "Miss Bitter," and "Mr. 'Gator," in *Let's Marry Said the Cherry and Other Nonsense Poems.* Copyright © 1974 by N. M. Bodecker. A Margaret K. McElderry Book. • *Myra Cohn Livingston.* "Father," and "12 October," in *The Malibu and Other Poems.* Copyright © 1972 by Myra Cohn Livingston. A Margaret K. McElderry Book. "Car Wash," and "The Tape," in *The Way Things Are and Other Poems.* Copyright © 1974 by Myra Cohn Livingston. A Margaret K. McElderry Book. • *Lilian Moore.* "Bedtime Stories," in *See My Lovely Poison Ivy.* Copyright © 1975 by Lilian Moore. "Until I Saw the Sea," in *I Feel the Same Way.* Copyright © 1967 by Lilian Moore. • *Mary O'Neill.* "Sound of Water," in *What Is That Sound!* Copyright © 1966 by Mary O'Neill. Reprinted with the permission of Atheneum Publishers. • *Artis Bernard.* "Snowfall" by Artis Bernard. Used with permission of the author. • *Rosemary Carr and Stephen Vincent Benét.* "Nancy Hanks" from *A Book of Americans.* A Book of Americans by Rosemary Carr and Stephen Vincent Benét. Holt, Rinehart and Winston. Copyright, 1933 by Rosemary and Stephen Vincent Benét. Copyright renewed © 1961 by Rosemary Carr Benét. Reprinted by permission of Brandt & Brandt Literary Agents, Inc. • *Miriam Chaikin.* "Light Another Candle," and "One-Upmanship," by Miriam Chaikin. Used by permission of the author. • *Marchette Chute.* "Day Before Christmas," from *Rhymes About the Country* by Marchette Chute. Copyright 1941 (Macmillan); renewed 1969. Reprinted by permission of the author. • *Freya Littledale.* "When My Dog Died," from *I Was Thinking* by Freya Littledale. Text Copyright © 1979 by Freya Littledale. Reprinted by permission of Curtis Brown, Ltd. • *Stephanie Calmenson.* "Tree Toad" by Stephanie Calmenson from *Never Take a Pig to Lunch,* copyright © 1982 by Stephanie Calmenson. • *Madeleine Edmondson.* Spells excerpted from chapters 6 and 9 of *Anna Witch* by Madeleine Edmondson. Copyright © 1982 by Madeleine Edmondson. Reprinted by permission of Doubleday & Company, Inc. • *Rachel Field.* "The Dancing Bear" from *Taxis and Toadstools* by Rachel Field. Copyright 1924 by Yale University Press. Reprinted by permission of Doubleday & Company, Inc. • *Rose Fyleman.* "Mice" from *Fifty-one Nursery Rhymes* by Rose Fyleman. Copyright 1932 by Doubleday & Company, Inc. Reprinted by permission of the publisher. • *Mary O'Neill.* "What Is Black?" from *Hailstones and Halibut Bones* by Mary O'Neill. Copyright © 1960 by The Curtis Publishing Company. Reprinted by permission of Doubleday & Company, Inc. • *Rhoda W. Bacmeister.* "Galoshes" from *Stories to Begin*

For my daughter, Rachel
with love

Contents

Introduction · 15

FIRST POEMS OF CHILDHOOD · 17

Do the Baby Cake-walk *Clyde Watson* · 19
Hoppity *A. A. Milne* · 19
There *Once* Was a Puffin *Florence Page Jaques* · 20
The Little Turtle *Vachel Lindsay* · 22
Little Black Bug *Margaret Wise Brown* · 23
The House of the Mouse *Lucy Sprague Mitchell* · 24
The Old Woman *Beatrix Potter* · 24
The City Mouse and the Garden Mouse
   Christina Georgina Rossetti · 25
The More It Snows *A. A. Milne* · 26
The Mitten Song *Marie Louise Allen* · 27
Galoshes *Rhoda Bacmeister* · 28
Rain *Robert Louis Stevenson* · 29
Daffadowndilly *Mother Goose* · 29
Mud *Polly Chase Boyden* · 30
On This Day *M. B. Goffstein* · 31
Down! Down! *Eleanor Farjeon* · 31
The Star *Jane Taylor* · 32
Wishing Poem *Traditional* · 32
I See the Moon *Author Unknown* · 33
Teddy Bear, Teddy Bear *Author Unknown* · 33
Song of the Train *David McCord* · 34
Dilly Dilly Piccalilli *Clyde Watson* · 36
If All the World Were Paper *Author Unknown* · 36
I Saw a Ship A-sailing *Mother Goose* · 37
The Cupboard *Walter de la Mare* · 38
This Little House Is Sugar *Langston Hughes* · 38
Baby's Drinking Song *James Kirkup* · 39
Mix a Pancake *Christina Georgina Rossetti* · 39
The Little Elf *John Kendrick Bangs* · 40
Wynken, Blynken, and Nod *Eugene Field* · 42
Rock, Rock, Sleep, My Baby *Clyde Watson* · 44

PEOPLE AND PORTRAITS · 45

Some People   *Rachel Field* · 47
Tired Tim   *Walter de la Mare* · 47
When Father Carves the Duck   *E. V. Wright* · 48
Mother to Son   *Langston Hughes* · 50
Husbands and Wives   *Miriam Hershenson* · 51
Little   *Dorothy Aldis* · 52
Moochie   *Eloise Greenfield* · 52
Two in Bed   *Abram Bunn Ross* · 53
My Sister Laura   *Spike Milligan* · 53
When Young Melissa Sweeps   *Nancy Byrd Turner* · 54
One-upmanship   *Miriam Chaikin* · 55
Fernando   *Marci Ridlon* · 56
Harvey Always Wins   *Jack Prelutsky* · 57
Catherine   *Karla Kuskin* · 58
Miss T.   *Walter de la Mare* · 59
Hug o' War   *Shel Silverstein* · 60

ANIMAL FAIR · 61

Animal Fair   *Author Unknown* · 63
At the Zoo   *William Makepeace Thackeray* · 64
Epigram Engraved on the Collar of a Dog
   Alexander Pope · 65
On Buying a Dog   *Edgar Klauber* · 66
Kindness to Animals   *Laura E. Richards* · 67
from Catalogue   *Rosalie Moore* · 68
Cat in the Snow   *Aileen Fisher* · 69
Listening   *Aileen Fisher* · 69
Mice   *Rose Fyleman* · 70
The Frog   *Hilaire Belloc* · 71
Crickets   *David McCord* · 72
Glowworm   *David McCord* · 72
Firefly   *Elizabeth Madox Roberts* · 73
The Tickle Rhyme   *Ian Serraillier* · 73
Bats   *Randall Jarrell* · 74
from A Bird   *Emily Dickinson* · 76
The Wren   *Issa* · 76
The Little Birds   *Author Unknown* · 76
The Eagle   *Alfred, Lord Tennyson* · 77
Duck   *Valerie Worth* · 78

Mrs. Peck-Pigeon *Eleanor Farjeon* • 78
The Toucan *Pyke Johnson, Jr.* • 79
Duck's Ditty *Kenneth Grahame* • 80
Holding Hands *Lenore M. Link* • 81
The Dancing Bear *Rachel Field* • 82
The Cow *Robert Louis Stevenson* • 83
Cows *James Reeves* • 84
Dinosaurs *Valerie Worth* • 86

SILLY TIME • 87

Bad and Good *Alexander Resnikoff* • 89
Soft-boiled Egg *Russell Hoban* • 89
The Eel *Ogden Nash* • 89
from Adventures of Isabel *Ogden Nash* • 90
Miss Bitter *N. M. Bodecker* • 92
Mr. 'Gator *N. M. Bodecker* • 93
Tip-toe Tail *Dixie Willson* • 94
Hippopotamus *Joanna Cole* • 95
The Last Cry of the Damp Fly *Dennis Lee* • 96
The Frog *Author Unknown* • 96
Tree Toad *Author Unknown* • 97
Jump-rope Rhyme *Traditional* • 98
Hand-clapping Rhyme *Traditional* • 98
'Tis Midnight *Author Unknown* • 99
The Perfect Reactionary *Hughes Mearns* • 100
The Old Sussex Road *Ian Serraillier* • 100
The Purple Cow *Gelett Burgess* • 101
As I Was Standing in the Street *Author Unknown* • 101
Nicholas Ned *Author Unknown* • 101
Eletelephony *Laura E. Richards* • 102
W *James Reeves* • 102
Ice Cream Chant *Traditional* • 103
Fuzzy Wuzzy Was a Bear *Traditional* • 103
A B C D Goldfish *Traditional* • 103
The Owl and the Pussy-cat *Edward Lear* • 104
Riddle Rhymes • 106 – 107
The Lazy People *Shel Silverstein* • 108
The Rain It Raineth *Charles Bowen* • 108
Friendship *Shel Silverstein* • 108
Get Up, Get Up *Author Unknown* • 109
Willie the Poisoner *Author Unknown* • 109

A Horse and a Flea and Three Blind Mice
  Author Unknown · *109*
I Eat My Peas with Honey *Author Unknown* · *109*
Disobedience *A. A. Milne* · *110*
Not Me *Shel Silverstein* · *114*
Old Man With a Beard *Edward Lear* · *114*
Old Man from Darjeeling *Author Unknown* · *115*
Old Man from Peru *Author Unknown* · *115*
An Epicure, Dining at Crewe *Author Unknown* · *117*
Jabberwocky *Lewis Carroll* · *118*
One, Two, Three—Gough! *Eve Merriam* · *120*

COME PLAY WITH ME · *121*

The Pickety Fence *David McCord* · *123*
Every Time I Climb a Tree *David McCord* · *124*
At the Sea-side *Robert Louis Stevenson* · *125*
Play *Frank Asch* · *126*
The Swing *Robert Louis Stevenson* · *127*
The Land of Counterpane *Robert Louis Stevenson* · *128*
Block City *Robert Louis Stevenson* · *129*
Where Go the Boats? *Robert Louis Stevenson* · *130*
Narcissa *Gwendolyn Brooks* · *131*
Little Jumping Joan *Mother Goose* · *131*
I Can Fly *Felice Holman* · *132*
Summer *Frank Asch* · *133*
The Base Stealer *Robert Francis* · *134*
The Sidewalk Racer, or On the Skateboard
  Lillian Morrison · *135*
Hide and Seek *Robert Graves* · *136*

WHEN I WENT OUT TO SEE THE SUN · *137*

Stopping by Woods on a Snowy Evening *Robert Frost* · *139*
Snowfall *Artis Bernard* · *140*
I Heard a Bird Sing *Oliver Herford* · *141*
First Sight *Philip Larkin* · *142*
Pippa's Song *Robert Browning* · *143*
Written in March *William Wordsworth* · *143*
I Bended unto Me *T. E. Brown* · *144*
April Rain Song *Langston Hughes* · *145*

When I Went Out   *Karla Kuskin*   •   145
That Was Summer   *Marci Ridlon*   •   146
Sound of Water   *Mary O'Neill*   •   148
Until I Saw the Sea   *Lilian Moore*   •   149
The Horses of the Sea   *Christina Georgina Rossetti*   •   150
The Night Will Never Stay   *Eleanor Farjeon*   •   150
Who Has Seen the Wind?   *Christina Georgina Rossetti*   •   151
Leaves   *Frank Asch*   •   152
Something Told the Wild Geese   *Rachel Field*   •   154

CELEBRATE THE TIME   •   155

Happy New Year, Anyway   *Joanna Cole*   •   157
Song   *William Shakespeare*   •   158
Valentine   *Donald Hall*   •   159
Jenny Kiss'd Me   *Leigh Hunt*   •   160
Phoebe in a Rosebush   *Clyde Watson*   •   160
Nancy Hanks 1784 – 1818   *Rosemary Carr and
    Stephen Vincent Benét*   •   161
Which Washington?   *Eve Merriam*   •   162
On Mother's Day   *Aileen Fisher*   •   163
Father   *Myra Cohn Livingston*   •   164
Fireworks   *Valerie Worth*   •   165
12 October   *Myra Cohn Livingston*   •   166
It's Halloween   *Jack Prelutsky*   •   167
Listen!   *Lilian Moore*   •   168
Bedtime Stories   *Lilian Moore*   •   169
Skeleton Parade   *Jack Prelutsky*   •   170
Witches' Spells   *Madeleine Edmondson*   •   171
Things That Go Bump in the Night   *Old Spell*   •   171
The Dark House   *Author Unknown*   •   172
The Goblin   *Rose Fyleman*   •   172
The First Thanksgiving   *Jack Prelutsky*   •   173
Thanksgiving Day   *Lydia Maria Child*   •   174
Light Another Candle   *Miriam Chaikin*   •   175
Little Tree   *e. e. cummings*   •   177
Christmas Is A-coming   *English Nursery Rhyme*   •   178
Day Before Christmas   *Marchette Chute*   •   178
A Visit from St. Nicholas   *Clement Clarke Moore*   •   179
I Heard the Bells on Christmas Day
    Henry Wadsworth Longfellow   •   182

A DIFFERENT WAY OF SEEING · 183

Houses   Aileen Fisher · 185
The Moon's the North Wind's Cooky   Vachel Lindsay · 186
The Garden Hose   Beatrice Janosco · 186
Conversation   Buson · 187
Steam Shovel   Charles Malam · 187
About an Excavation   Charles Reznikoff · 187
The Stranger in the Pumpkin   John Ciardi · 188
Chairs   Valerie Worth · 189
The Tape   Myra Cohn Livingston · 190
Surf   Lillian Morrison · 191
Waking from a Nap on the Beach   May Swenson · 191
What Is Black?   Mary O'Neill · 193
Sunflakes   Frank Asch · 194
Rocks   Florence Parry Heide · 194
Car Wash   Myra Cohn Livingston · 195
Southbound on the Freeway   May Swenson · 196

INSIDE MYSELF · 197

At Annika's Place   Siv Widerberg · 199
Best?   Siv Widerberg · 200
Where Have You Been Dear?   Karla Kuskin · 201
The Question   Karla Kuskin · 202
In the Library   Michael Patrick Hearn · 203
Eviction   Lucille Clifton · 203
Zinnias   Valerie Worth · 204
Incident   Countee Cullen · 205
Listening to Grownups Quarreling   Ruth Whitman · 206
Poem   Langston Hughes · 207
When My Dog Died   Freya Littledale · 208
Crying   Galway Kinnell · 209
Jigsaw Puzzle   Russell Hoban · 210
A Riddle   Charlotte Zolotow · 210
A Story That Could Be True   William Stafford · 211
Once   Siv Widerberg · 212
Afternoon on a Hill   Edna St. Vincent Millay · 212
Blessèd Lord, What It Is to Be Young   David McCord · 213
The Sun   John Drinkwater · 213
This Is My Rock   David McCord · 214

Introduction

Long ago I read that the word "anthology"—a rather dull word, I thought, for a collection of poems or tales—came from the Greek for "flower gathering." This image was with me as I picked the poems for this book, for it seemed to describe my work, except that flowers do not speak and poems are made to be listened to.

Some of the poems here are favorites remembered from childhood, and many are new discoveries, but every one has special meaning for me. I have not tried to make an "objective" collection, including all the classic and contemporary poems that children "ought" to know. Instead, I have chosen poetry that made me stop, feeling full of the brightness of the images or the joyousness of the rhythm or the recognition of a hidden feeling. When I felt myself lifted above the ordinary, I had the impulse to share the experience with others.

I have put these poems together as a family collection, one that will grow with a child and be enjoyed by older and younger sisters and brothers. Preschool children will find many poems to like in the first chapter of the book, which has been planned especially for them. But there are no rules against adventuring into the other chapters, which are organized by subjects, with school-age children in mind.

The important thing is that there are poems for everyone in every mood—for parents to read to children, for children to read aloud, for teachers to share with classes, and for everyone to return to alone. So pick a poem and listen to it now.

JOANNA COLE

First Poems of Childhood

Very young children are attracted by the subject of a poem or the vivid images in it, but most of all they are attracted by its music. Little children will ask again for a poem that has strong rhythm and rhyme and words that sound like the things they describe.

Try David McCord's "Song of the Train" and see how the refrain, with its pattern of "clickety-clacks," does indeed become the "song of the track." And notice how "Baby's Drinking Song" by James Kirkup seems to rollick along from the first "little" to the last. I always find myself saying it all in one breath and then laughing at the end.

If you are reading poems to a small child, try introducing each one, simply asking something like, "Here is one about a mouse. Shall we read it?" Even more enticing for the child is the chance to say the poem or parts of it along with you. A good one to start with is "The More It Snows" from A. A. Milne's book *The House at Pooh Corner.* You can say the poem while your listener chimes in with the "tiddely-poms" —just as Pooh and Piglet did in the story.

DO THE BABY CAKE-WALK

Do the baby cake-walk
A one-step, a two-step
A wobble & a bobble in the knee,
With a toe heel toe
And a giddy-go-round you go
Won't you do the baby cake-walk
For me?

CLYDE WATSON

HOPPITY

Christopher Robin goes
Hoppity, hoppity,
Hoppity, hoppity, hop.
Whenever I tell him
Politely to stop it, he
Says he can't possibly stop.
If he stopped hopping, he couldn't go anywhere,
Poor little Christopher
Couldn't go anywhere...
That's why he *always* goes
Hoppity, hoppity,
Hoppity,
Hoppity,
Hop.   A. A. MILNE

THERE ONCE WAS A PUFFIN

Oh, there once was a Puffin
Just the shape of a muffin,
And he lived on an island
In the
   bright
     blue
       sea!

He ate little fishes,
That were most delicious,
And he had them for supper
And he
   had
     them
       for tea.

But this poor little Puffin,
He couldn't play nothin',
For he hadn't anybody
To
   play
     with
       at all.

So he sat on his island,
And he cried for a while, and
He felt very lonely,
And he
  felt
    very
      small.

Then along came the fishes,
And they said, "If you wishes,
You can have us for playmates,
Instead
  of
    for
      tea!"

So they now play together,
In all sorts of weather,
And the puffin eats pancakes,
Like you
  and
    like
      me.

THE LITTLE TURTLE

There was a little turtle.
He lived in a box.
He swam in a puddle.
He climbed on the rocks.

He snapped at a mosquito.
He snapped at a flea.
He snapped at a minnow.
And he snapped at me.

He caught the mosquito.
He caught the flea.
He caught the minnow.
But he didn't catch me.

VACHEL LINDSAY

LITTLE BLACK BUG

Little black bug,
Little black bug,
Where have you been?
I've been under the rug,
Said the little black bug.
Bug-ug-ug-ug.

Little green fly,
Little green fly,
Where have you been?
I've been way up high,
Said little green fly.
Bzzzzzzz.

Little old mouse,
Little old mouse,
Where have you been?
I've been all through the house,
Said little old mouse.
Squeak-eak-eak-eak-eak.

MARGARET WISE BROWN

THE HOUSE OF THE MOUSE

The house of the mouse
is a wee little house,
a green little house in the grass,
which big clumsy folk
may hunt and may poke
and still never see as they pass
this sweet little, neat little,
wee little, green little,
cuddle-down hide-away
house in the grass.

LUCY SPRAGUE MITCHELL

THE OLD WOMAN

You know the old woman
    Who lived in a shoe?
And had so many children
    She didn't know what to do?

I think if she lived in
    A little shoe-house—
That little old woman was
    Surely a mouse!

BEATRIX POTTER

THE CITY MOUSE AND THE GARDEN MOUSE

The city mouse lives in a house;
  The garden mouse lives in a bower,
He's friendly with the frogs and toads,
  And sees the pretty plants in flower.

The city mouse eats bread and cheese;
  The garden mouse eats what he can;
We will not grudge him seeds and stalks,
  Poor little, timid, furry man.

CHRISTINA GEORGINA ROSSETTI

THE MORE IT SNOWS

The more it
SNOWS-tiddely-pom,
The more it
GOES-tiddely-pom
The more it
GOES-tiddely-pom
On
Snowing.

And nobody
KNOWS-tiddely-pom,
How cold my
TOES-tiddely-pom
How cold my
TOES-tiddely-pom
Are
Growing.

A. A. MILNE

THE MITTEN SONG

"Thumbs in the thumb-place,
Fingers all together!"
This is the song
We sing in mitten-weather.
When it is cold,
It doesn't matter whether
Mittens are wool,
Or made of finest leather.
This is the song
We sing in mitten-weather:
"Thumbs in the thumb-place,
Fingers all together!"

MARIE LOUISE ALLEN

GALOSHES

Susie's galoshes
Make splishes and sploshes
And slooshes and sloshes
As Susie steps slowly
Along in the slush.

They stamp and they tramp
On the ice and concrete,
They get stuck in the muck and the mud;
But Susie likes much best to hear

The slippery slush
As it slooshes and sloshes,
And splishes and sploshes,
All around her galoshes!

RHODA BACMEISTER

RAIN

The rain is raining all around,
  It falls on field and tree,
It rains on the umbrellas here,
  And on the ships at sea.

ROBERT LOUIS STEVENSON

DAFFADOWNDILLY

Daffadowndilly
  Has come up to town,
In a yellow petticoat
  And a green gown.

MOTHER GOOSE

MUD

Mud is very nice to feel
All squishy-squash between the toes!
I'd rather wade in wiggly mud
Than smell a yellow rose.

Nobody else but the rosebush knows
How nice mud feels
Between the toes.

POLLY CHASE BOYDEN

ON THIS DAY

On this day
I'm going to pick
a big bouquet
and put it in my shoe
and let it sail away.
And when it gets
across the sea,
how amazed the children
there
will be.

M. B. GOFFSTEIN

DOWN! DOWN!

Down, down!
Yellow and brown
The leaves are falling over the town.

ELEANOR FARJEON

31

THE STAR

Twinkle, twinkle, little star,
How I wonder what you are!
Up above the world so high,
Like a diamond in the sky.

JANE TAYLOR

WISHING POEM

Star light, star bright,
First star I've seen tonight,
Wish I may, wish I might,
Have this wish I wish tonight.

TRADITIONAL

I SEE THE MOON

I see the moon,
And the moon sees me.
God bless the moon,
And God bless me.

AUTHOR UNKNOWN

TEDDY BEAR, TEDDY BEAR

Teddy Bear, Teddy Bear,
Go upstairs.
Teddy Bear, Teddy Bear,
Say your prayers.
Teddy Bear, Teddy Bear,
Turn out the light.
Teddy Bear, Teddy Bear,
Say good night.

AUTHOR UNKNOWN

SONG OF THE TRAIN

Clickety-clack,
Wheels on the track,
This is the way
They begin the attack:
Click-ety-clack,
Click-ety-clack,
Click-ety-*clack*-ety,
Click-ety
Clack.

Clickety-clack,
Over the crack,
Faster and faster
The song of the track:
Clickety-clack,
Clickety-clack,
Clickety, clackety,
Clackety
Clack.

Riding in front,
Riding in back,
Everyone hears
The song of the track:
Clickety-clack,
Clickety-clack,
Clickety, *clickety*,
Clackety
Clack.

DAVID McCORD

DILLY DILLY PICCALILLI

Dilly Dilly Piccalilli
Tell me something very silly:
There was a chap his name was Bert
He ate the buttons off his shirt.

CLYDE WATSON

IF ALL THE WORLD WERE PAPER

If all the world were paper,
And all the sea were ink,
And all the trees were bread and cheese,
What should we do for drink?

AUTHOR UNKNOWN

I SAW A SHIP A-SAILING

I saw a ship a-sailing,
A-sailing on the sea;
And, oh! it was all laden
With pretty things for thee!

There were comfits in the cabin,
And apples in the hold;
The sails were made of silk,
And the masts were made of gold.

The four-and-twenty sailors
That stood between the decks,
Were four-and-twenty white mice
With chains about their necks.

The captain was a duck,
With a packet on his back;
And when the ship began to move,
The captain said, "Quack! Quack!"

MOTHER GOOSE

THE CUPBOARD

I know a little cupboard,
With a teeny tiny key,
And there's a jar of Lollipops
    For me, me, me.

It has a little shelf, my dear,
As dark as dark can be,
And there's a dish of Banbury Cakes
    For me, me, me.

I have a small fat grandmamma,
With a very slippery knee,
And she's Keeper of the Cupboard,
    With the key, key, key.

And when I'm very good, my dear,
As good as good can be,
There's Banbury Cakes, and Lollipops
    For me, me, me.

WALTER DE LA MARE

THIS LITTLE HOUSE IS SUGAR

This little house is sugar,
Its roof with snow is piled,
And from its tiny window
Peeps a maple-sugar child.

LANGSTON HUGHES

38

BABY'S DRINKING SONG

Sip a little
Sup a little
From your little
Cup a little
Sup a little
Sip a little
Put it to your
Lip a little
Tip a little
Tap a little
Not into your
Lap or it'll
Drip a little
Drop a little
On the table
Top a little.

JAMES KIRKUP

MIX A PANCAKE

Mix a pancake,
Stir a pancake,
    Pop it in the pan;
Fry the pancake,
Toss the pancake, —
    Catch it if you can.

CHRISTINA GEORGINA ROSSETTI

THE LITTLE ELF

I met a little Elf-man, once,
   Down where the lilies blow.
I asked him why he was so small,
   And why he didn't grow.

He slightly frowned, and with his eye
   He looked me through and through.
"I'm quite as big for me," said he,
   "As you are big for you."

JOHN KENDRICK BANGS

WYNKEN, BLYNKEN, AND NOD

Wynken, Blynken, and Nod one night
   Sailed off in a wooden shoe,—
Sailed on a river of crystal light
   Into a sea of dew.
"Where are you going, and what do you wish?"
   The old moon asked the three.
"We have come to fish for the herring fish
   That live in this beautiful sea;
   Nets of silver and gold have we!"
         Said Wynken,
         Blynken,
         And Nod.

The old moon laughed and sang a song,
   As they rocked in the wooden shoe;
And the wind that sped them all night long
   Ruffled the waves of dew.
The little stars were the herring fish
   That lived in that beautiful sea—
"Now cast your nets wherever you wish,—
   Never afeard are we!"
   So cried the stars to the fishermen three,
         Wynken,
         Blynken,
         And Nod.

All night long their nets they threw
  To the stars in the twinkling foam,—
Then down from the skies came the wooden shoe,
  Bringing the fishermen home:
'Twas all so pretty a sail, it seemed
  As if it could not be;
And some folk thought 'twas a dream they'd dreamed
  Of sailing that beautiful sea;
  But I shall name you the fishermen three:
        Wynken,
        Blynken,
        And Nod.

Wynken and Blynken are two little eyes,
  And Nod is a little head,
And the wooden shoe that sailed the skies
  Is a wee one's trundle-bed;
So shut your eyes while Mother sings
  Of wonderful sights that be,
And you shall see the beautiful things
  As you rock in the misty sea
  Where the old shoe rocked the fishermen three:—
        Wynken,
        Blynken,
        And Nod.

EUGENE FIELD

ROCK, ROCK, SLEEP, MY BABY

Rock, rock, sleep, my baby
Sings the sweet cuckoo...
When your Daddy comes back home
He'll bring a toy for you.

Hush, hush, sleep, my baby
Sleep the whole night through...
When your Daddy comes back home
He'll sing a song for you.

CLYDE WATSON

44

People and Portraits

"Isn't it strange," the poet asks, "some people make you feel so tired inside?" But others can make you feel quite different—cheerful, loved, amused, even furious.

In just a few lines a poet can paint a portrait of a person. Reading "When Young Melissa Sweeps" by Nancy Byrd Turner, can't you almost see a girl who "dances with the broom"? And haven't you known a likable show-off like Marci Ridlon's Fernando or an *un*likable guy like the Harvey that Jack Prelutsky writes about?

One poem, "Two in Bed" by Abram Bunn Ross, describes a little brother two ways: in words, saying that he sleeps doubled up like a V, and also in the shape of the poem, which is arranged to form a V. Look for yourself and see.

SOME PEOPLE

Isn't it strange some people make
   You feel so tired inside,
Your thoughts begin to shrivel up
   Like leaves all brown and dried!

But when you're with some other ones,
   It's stranger still to find
Your thoughts as thick as fireflies
   All shiny in your mind!

RACHEL FIELD

TIRED TIM

Poor tired Tim! It's sad for him.
He lags the long bright morning through,
Ever so tired of nothing to do;
He moons and mopes the livelong day,
Nothing to think about, nothing to say;
Up to bed with his candle to creep,
Too tired to yawn, too tired to sleep:
Poor tired Tim! It's sad for him.

WALTER DE LA MARE

WHEN FATHER CARVES THE DUCK

We all look on with anxious eyes
   When Father carves the duck,
And Mother almost always sighs
   When Father carves the duck;
Then all of us prepare to rise,
And hold our bibs before our eyes,
And be prepared for some surprise,
   When Father carves the duck.

He braces up and grabs a fork
   Whene'er he carves a duck,
And won't allow a soul to talk
   Until he's carved the duck;
The fork is jabbed into the sides,
Across the breast the knife he slides,
While every careful person hides
   From flying chips of duck.

The platter's always sure to slip
    When Father carves a duck,
And how it makes the dishes skip!
    Potatoes fly amuck!
The squash and cabbage leap in space,
We get some gravy in our face,
And Father mutters Hindoo grace
    Whene'er he carves a duck.

We then have learned to walk around
    The dining room and pluck
From off the window sills and walls
    Our share of Father's duck,
While Father growls and blows and jaws
And swears the knife was full of flaws,
And Mother laughs at him because
    He couldn't carve a duck.

E. V. WRIGHT

MOTHER TO SON

Well, son, I'll tell you:
Life for me ain't been no crystal stair.
It's had tacks in it,
And splinters,
And boards torn up,
And places with no carpet on the floor—
Bare.
But all the time
I'se been a-climbin' on,
And reachin' landin's,
And turnin' corners,
And sometimes goin' in the dark
Where there ain't been no light.
So, boy, don't you turn back.
Don't you set down on the steps
'Cause you finds it kinder hard.
Don't you fall now—
For I'se still goin', honey,
I'se still climbin',
And life for me ain't been no crystal stair.

LANGSTON HUGHES

HUSBANDS AND WIVES

Husbands and wives
    With children between them
Sit in the subway;
    So I have seen them.

One word only
    From station to station;
So much talk for
    So close a relation.

MIRIAM HERSHENSON

LITTLE

I am the sister of him
  And he is my brother.
He is too little for us
  To talk to each other.

So every morning I show him
  My doll and my book;
But every morning he still is
  Too little to look.

DOROTHY ALDIS

MOOCHIE

Moochie likes to keep on playing
That same old silly game
Peeka   Boo!
Peeka   Boo!

I get tired of it
But it makes her laugh
And every time she laughs
She gets the hiccups
And every time she gets the hiccups
I laugh

ELOISE GREENFIELD

TWO IN BED

When my brother Tommy
Sleeps in bed with me,
He doubles up
And makes
himself
exactly
like
a
V

And 'cause the bed is not so wide,
A part of him is on my side.

ABRAM BUNN ROSS

MY SISTER LAURA

My sister Laura's bigger than me
And lifts me up quite easily.
I can't lift her, I've tried and tried;
She must have something heavy inside.

SPIKE MILLIGAN

53

WHEN YOUNG MELISSA SWEEPS

When young Melissa sweeps a room
I vow she dances with the broom!

She curtsies in a corner brightly
And leads her partner forth politely.

Then up and down in jigs and reels,
With gold dust flying at their heels,

They caper. With a whirl or two
They make the wainscot shine like new;

They waltz beside the hearth, and quick
It brightens, shabby brick by brick.

A gay gavotte across the floor,
A Highland fling from door to door,

And every crack and corner's clean
Enough to suit a dainty queen.

If ever you are full of gloom,
Just watch Melissa sweep a room!

NANCY BYRD TURNER

ONE-UPMANSHIP

"I bet I can hold my breath
longer than you," said Lou.

"Oh, yeah? I bet you can't.
Let's see," said Sue.

Lou took a breath.
He held it for a minute,
he held it for two,
he held it and held it
till his face turned blue.

Suddenly—WHOOSH!—went Lou.
He took off for the sky
like a rocket shot
on the Fourth of July.

Sue looked up,
watching Lou disappear.
"You win," she called,
but Lou didn't hear.

MIRIAM CHAIKIN

FERNANDO

Fernando has a basketball.
He tap, tap, taps it down the hall,
then leaps up high and shoots with care.
The fact a basket isn't there
he totally dismisses.
He says he never misses.
My crazy friend Fernando.

MARCI RIDLON

HARVEY ALWAYS WINS

Every game that Harvey plays,
Harvey always wins,
everybody knows he will
before the game begins.

Follow the leader, leapfrog, tag,
whatever game we choose,
as long as Harvey's in the game
then Harvey doesn't lose.

We hate to play with Harvey,
he loves to spoil our fun,
as soon as a game is over
he shouts, "You see, I won."

Harvey's always showing off,
he wins when he competes,
it isn't that he's better,
it's that Harvey always cheats.

JACK PRELUTSKY

CATHERINE

Catherine said, "I think I'll bake
A most delicious chocolate cake."
She took some mud and mixed it up
While adding water from a cup
And then some weeds and nuts and bark
And special gravel from the park
A thistle and a dash of sand.
She beat out all the lumps by hand.
And on the top she wrote "To You"
The way she says the bakers do
And then she signed it "Fondly, C."
And gave the whole of it to me.
I thanked her but I wouldn't dream
Of eating cake without ice cream.

KARLA KUSKIN

MISS T.

It's a very odd thing—
   As odd as can be—
That whatever Miss T. eats
   Turns into Miss T.;
Porridge and apples,
   Mince, muffins, and mutton,
Jam, junket, jumbles—
   Not a rap, not a button
It matters; the moment
   They're out of her plate,
Though shared by Miss Butcher
   And sour Mr. Bate,
Tiny and cheerful,
   And neat as can be,
Whatever Miss T. eats
   Turns into Miss T.

WALTER DE LA MARE

59

HUG O' WAR

I will not play at tug o' war.
I'd rather play at hug o' war,
Where everyone hugs
Instead of tugs,
Where everyone giggles
And rolls on the rug,
Where everyone kisses,
And everyone grins,
And everyone cuddles,
And everyone wins.

SHEL SILVERSTEIN

Animal Fair

The poems I like best about animals are the ones that describe something familiar in a new way. For instance, in his poem about a field of chirping crickets, David McCord calls them "ticket-takers" because they sound like so many conductors punching tickets on a train. In the poem "Catalogue" Rosalie Moore says, "Cats sleep fat and walk thin." If you have a cat, you know this is true, but you probably never thought to say it exactly that way.

Sometimes a poem can change the way we see an animal. I never feed white ducks in a pond without thinking they are like toys with "yellow rubber-skinned feet"—the way they are described in Valerie Worth's poem "Duck."

ANIMAL FAIR

I went to the animal fair,
The birds and beasts were there.
The big baboon by the light of the moon
Was combing his auburn hair.

The monkey he got drunk.
He stepped on the elephant's trunk.
The elephant sneezed
And fell on his knees,
And that was the end of the monk,
     the monk, the monk.
And that was the end of the monk.

AUTHOR UNKNOWN

AT THE ZOO

First I saw the white bear,
   Then I saw the black;
Then I saw the camel
   With a hump upon his back;
Then I saw the grey wolf,
   With mutton in his maw;
Then I saw a wombat
   Waddle in the straw;
Then I saw the elephant
   A-waving of his trunk;
Then I saw the monkeys—
   Mercy, how unpleasantly they—
Smelt!

WILLIAM MAKEPEACE THACKERAY

EPIGRAM ENGRAVED ON THE COLLAR OF A DOG
Which I Gave to His Royal Highness

I am his Highness' dog at Kew;
Pray tell me, sir, whose dog are you?

ALEXANDER POPE

ON BUYING A DOG

"I wish to buy a dog," she said,
"A dog you're sure is quite well bred,
In fact, I'd like some guarantee
He's favored with a pedigree."

"My charming friend," the pet man said,
"I have a dog that's so well bred,
If he could talk, I'll guarantee
He'd never speak to you or me."

EDGAR KLAUBER

KINDNESS TO ANIMALS

Riddle cum diddle cum dido,
My little dog's name is Fido;
    I bought him a wagon,
    And hitched up a dragon,
And off we both went for a ride, oh!

Riddle cum diddle cum doodle,
My little cat's name is Toodle;
    I curled up her hair,
    But she only said, "There!
You have made me look just like a poodle!"

Riddle cum diddle cum dinky,
My little pig's name is Winkie;
    I keep him quite clean
    With the washing machine,
And I rinse him all off in the sinkie.

LAURA E. RICHARDS

from CATALOGUE

Cats sleep fat and walk thin.
Cats, when they sleep, slump;
When they wake, stretch and begin
Over, pulling their ribs in.
Cats walk thin...
Cats sleep fat.
They spread out comfort underneath them
Like a good mat,
As if they picked the place
And then sat;
You walk around one
As if he were the City Hall
After that.

ROSALIE MOORE

CAT IN THE SNOW

Stepping gingerly,
he goes
through the garden
when it snows,
hoping not
to wet his toes.
And I'm sure
he never knows
every footprint
is a rose.

AILEEN FISHER

LISTENING

When it's time
for milk or fish,
my cat hears any sound
of Dish.

But when he's sunning
and I call,
he seldom hears
my voice at all.

AILEEN FISHER

MICE

I think mice
Are rather nice.

Their tails are long,
Their faces small,
They haven't any
Chins at all.
Their ears are pink,
Their teeth are white,
They run about
The house at night.
They nibble things
They shouldn't touch
And no one seems
To like them much.

But I think mice
Are nice.

ROSE FYLEMAN

THE FROG

Be kind and tender to the Frog
   And do not call him names,
As "Slimy-skin," or "Polly-wog,"
   Or likewise "Ugly James,"
Or "Gap-a-grin," or "Toad-gone-wrong,"
   Or "Bill Bandy-knees":
The Frog is justly sensitive
   To epithets like these.
No animal will more repay
   A treatment kind and fair
At least so lonely people say
Who keep a frog (and, by the way,
They are extremely rare).

HILAIRE BELLOC

CRICKETS

all busy punching tickets,
clicking their little punches.
The tickets come in bunches,
good for a brief excursion,
good for a cricket's version
of travel (before it snows) to
the places a cricket goes to.
Alas! the crickets sing alas
in the dry September grass.
Alas, alas, in every acre,
every one a ticket-taker.

DAVID MCCORD

GLOWWORM

Never talk down to a glowworm—
Such as *What do you knowworm?*
How's it down belowworm?
Guess you're quite a slowworm.
No. Just say
            Helloworm!

DAVID MCCORD

FIREFLY
A Song

A little light is going by,
Is going up to see the sky,
A little light with wings.

I never could have thought of it,
To have a little bug all lit
And made to go on wings.

Elizabeth Madox Roberts

THE TICKLE RHYME

"Who's that tickling my back?" said the wall.
"Me," said a small
Caterpillar. "I'm learning
To crawl."

Ian Serraillier

BATS

A bat is born
Naked and blind and pale.
His mother makes a pocket of her tail
And catches him. He clings to her long fur
By his thumbs and toes and teeth.
And then the mother dances through the night
Doubling and looping, soaring, somersaulting—
Her baby hangs on underneath.
All night, in happiness, she hunts and flies.
Her high sharp cries
Like shining needlepoints of sound
Go out into the night and, echoing back,
Tell her what they have touched.
She hears how far it is, how big it is,
Which way it's going:
She lives by hearing.
The mother eats the moths and gnats she catches
In full flight; in full flight

The mother drinks the water of the pond
She skims across. Her baby hangs on tight.
Her baby drinks the milk she makes him
In moonlight or starlight, in mid-air.
Their single shadow, printed on the moon
Or fluttering across the stars,
Whirls on all night; at daybreak
The tired mother flaps home to her rafter.
The others all are there.
They hang themselves up by their toes,
They wrap themselves in their brown wings.
Bunched upside down, they sleep in air.
Their sharp ears, their sharp teeth, their quick sharp faces
Are dull and slow and mild.
All the bright day, as the mother sleeps,
She folds her wings about her sleeping child.

RANDALL JARRELL

from A BIRD

A bird came down the walk:
He did not know I saw;
He bit an angle-worm in halves
And ate the fellow, raw.

And then he drank a dew
From a convenient grass,
And then hopped sidewise to the wall
To let a beetle pass.

Emily Dickinson

THE WREN

The wren
Looking here, looking there,—
"Dropped something?"

Issa
Translated by R. H. Blyth

THE LITTLE BIRDS

The little birds sit in their nest and beg,
All mouth that once had been all egg.

Author Unknown

THE EAGLE

He clasps the crag with crooked hands;
Close to the sun in lonely lands,
Ringed with the azure world, he stands.

The wrinkled sea beneath him crawls;
He watches from his mountain walls,
And like a thunderbolt he falls.

ALFRED, LORD TENNYSON

DUCK

When the neat white
Duck walks like a toy
Out of the water
On yellow rubber-skinned feet,

And speaks wet sounds,
Hardly opening
His round-tipped wooden
Yellow-painted beak,

And wags his tail,
Flicking the last
Glass water-drops
From his flat china back,

Then we would like
To pick him up, take
Him home with us, put him
Away, on a shelf, to keep.

                    VALERIE WORTH

MRS. PECK-PIGEON

Mrs. Peck-Pigeon
Is picking for bread,
Bob-bob-bob
Goes her little round head.
Tame as a pussy-cat
In the street,
Step-step-step
Go her little red feet.
With her little red feet
And her little round head,
Mrs. Peck-Pigeon
Goes picking for bread.

ELEANOR FARJEON

THE TOUCAN

Of all the birds I know,
Few can
Boast of as big a bill as a
Toucan.
Yet I can think of one
Who can;
And if you think a while, too,
You can:
Another toucan in the
Zoo can.

PYKE JOHNSON, JR.

DUCK'S DITTY

All along the backwater,
   Through the rushes tall,
Ducks are a-dabbling,
   Up tails all!

Ducks' tails, drakes' tails,
   Yellow feet a-quiver,
Yellow bills all out of sight
   Busy in the river!

Slushy green undergrowth
   Where the roaches swim—
Here we keep our larder,
   Cool and full and dim.

Everyone for what he likes!
   We like to be
Heads down, tails up,
   Dabbling free!

High in the blue above
   Swifts whirl and call—
We are down a-dabbling,
   Up tails all!

KENNETH GRAHAME

HOLDING HANDS

Elephants walking
Along the trails

Are holding hands
By holding tails.

Trunks and tails
Are handy things

When elephants walk
In circus rings.

Elephants work
And elephants play

And elephants walk
And feel so gay.

And when they walk—
It never fails

They're holding hands
By holding tails.

LENORE M. LINK

THE DANCING BEAR

Slowly he turns himself round and round,
   Lifting his paws with care,
Twisting his head in a sort of bow
   To the people watching there.

His keeper, grinding a wheezy tune,
   Jerks at the iron chain,
And the dusty, patient bear goes through
   His solemn tricks again.

Only his eyes are still and fixed
   In a wide, bewildered stare,
More like a child's lost in woods at night
   Than the eyes of a big brown bear.

RACHEL FIELD

THE COW

The friendly cow all red and white,
    I love with all my heart;
She gives me cream with all her might,
    To eat with apple tart.

She wanders lowing here and there,
    And yet she cannot stray,
All in the pleasant open air,
    The pleasant light of day;

And blown by all the winds that pass
    And wet with all the showers,
She walks among the meadow grass
    And eats the meadow flowers.

ROBERT LOUIS STEVENSON

COWS

Half the time they munched the grass, and all the time they lay
Down in the water-meadows, the lazy month of May,
    A-chewing,
    A-mooing,
  To pass the hours away.

  "Nice weather," said the brown cow.
    "Ah," said the white.
  "Grass is very tasty."
    "Grass is all right."

Half the time they munched the grass, and all the time they lay
Down in the water-meadows, the lazy month of May,
    A-chewing,
    A-mooing,
  To pass the hours away.

  "Rain coming," said the brown cow.
    "Ah," said the white.
  "Flies is very tiresome."
    "Flies bite."

Half the time they munched the grass, and all the time they lay
Down in the water-meadows, the lazy month of May,
    A-chewing,
    A-mooing,
  To pass the hours away.

  "Time to go," said the brown cow.
    "Ah," said the white.
"Nice chat." "Very pleasant."
    "Night." "Night."

Half the time they munched the grass, and all the time they lay
Down in the water-meadows, the lazy month of May,
    A-chewing,
    A-mooing,
  To pass the hours away.

JAMES REEVES

DINOSAURS

Dinosaurs
Do not count,
Because
They are all
Dead:

None of us
Saw them, dogs
Do not even
Know that
They were there—

But they
Still walk
About heavily
In everybody's
Head.

VALERIE WORTH

Silly Time

You are probably much too old and serious for silly poems
like the ones that come next. So you might as well just skip
them.

What's that? You say you'll just read the first one to see if
it's funny? All right, but I bet you can't read just one!

BAD AND GOOD

Do you know what is bad?
I'll tell you what is bad:
To sprinkle catchup on your dad,
'Specially when he's mad.

Do you know what is good?
I'll tell you what is good:
To keep your foot out of your food
When mommy says you should.

ALEXANDER RESNIKOFF

SOFT-BOILED EGG

I do not like the way you slide,
I do not like your soft inside,
I do not like you lots of ways,
And I could do for many days
Without eggs.

RUSSELL HOBAN

THE EEL

I don't mind eels
Except as meals.
And the way they feels.

OGDEN NASH

from ADVENTURES OF ISABEL

Isabel met an enormous bear,
Isabel, Isabel, didn't care;
The bear was hungry, the bear was ravenous,
The bear's big mouth was cruel and cavernous.
The bear said, Isabel, glad to meet you,
How do, Isabel, now I'll eat you!
Isabel, Isabel, didn't worry,
Isabel didn't scream or scurry.
She washed her hands and she straightened her
    hair up,
Then Isabel quietly ate the bear up.

Once in a night as black as pitch
Isabel met a wicked old witch.
The witch's face was cross and wrinkled,
The witch's gums with teeth were sprinkled.
Ho ho, Isabel! the old witch crowed,
I'll turn you into an ugly toad!
Isabel, Isabel, didn't worry,
Isabel didn't scream or scurry.
She showed no rage and she showed no rancor,
But she turned the witch into milk and drank her.

Isabel met a hideous giant,
Isabel continued self-reliant.
The giant was hairy, the giant was horrid,
He had one eye in the middle of his forehead.
Good morning, Isabel, the giant said,
I'll grind your bones to make my bread.
Isabel, Isabel, didn't worry,
Isabel didn't scream or scurry.
She nibbled the zwieback that she always fed off,
And when it was gone, she cut the giant's head off.

OGDEN NASH

MISS BITTER

Sitter Bitter
(baby-sitter
Violet Amanda Bitter)
loved to sit,
but, rather sadly,
though the babies
loved her madly,
though they loved her
every bit,
never got
a chance to sit
since they found her
with her knitting,
since the day
they found her, sitting
knitting on the baby's knee,
having buttered toast and tea.
When they cried:
"AMANDA BITTER!
Most outrageous baby-sitter
BITTER! You get off that knee!"
she inquired:
"Want some tea?"

N. M. BODECKER

MR. 'GATOR

Elevator operator
P. Cornelius Alligator,
when his passengers
were many,
never
ever
passed up
any:
when his passengers
were few,
always managed
to make do.
When they told him:
"Mister 'Gator!
quickly
in your elevator
take us
to the nineteenth floor!"
they were never
seen no more.

N. M. Bodecker

TIP-TOE TAIL

A fish took a notion
To come from his ocean
And take in the sights of the town.
So he bought him a hat
And a coat and cravat
And a one-legged trouser of brown!
  He did!
And a one-legged trouser of brown!

His suit fit so queerly
That everyone nearly
Went following out on the street!
But the best of it all
Was how handsome and tall
He could walk when he didn't have feet!
  He did!
He walked when he didn't have feet!

Now I must confess that
I surely would guess that
A fish trying walking would fail.
But with no one's advice
He looked perfectly nice
On the very tip-toe of his tail!
  He did!
On the very tip-toe of his tail!

DIXIE WILLSON

94

HIPPOPOTAMUS

See the handsome hippopotamus,
Wading on the river-bottomus.
He goes everywhere he wishes
In pursuit of little fishes.
Cooks them in his cooking-potamus.
"My," fish say, "he eats a lot-of-us!"

JOANNA COLE

THE LAST CRY OF THE DAMP FLY

Bitter batter boop!
I'm swimming in your soup.

Bitter batter bout:
Kindly get me out!

Bitter batter boon:
Not upon your spoon!

Bitter batter bum!
Now I'm in your tum!

DENNIS LEE

THE FROG

What a wonderful bird the frog are—
When he stand, he sit almost;
When he hop, he fly almost.
He ain't got no sense hardly;
He ain't got no tail hardly either.
When he sit, he sit on what he ain't got almost.

AUTHOR UNKNOWN

96

TREE TOAD

A tree toad loved a she-toad
Who lived up in a tree.
He was a two-toed tree toad
But a three-toed toad was she.
The two-toed tree toad tried to win
The three-toed she-toad's heart,
For the two-toed tree toad loved the ground
That the three-toed tree toad trod.
But the two-toed tree toad tried in vain.
He couldn't please her whim.
From her tree toad bower
With her three-toed power
The she-toad vetoed him.

AUTHOR UNKNOWN
ADAPTED BY STEPHANIE CALMENSON

JUMP-ROPE RHYME

"Hello, hello, hello, sir,
Meet me at the grocer."
"No sir."
"Why sir?"
"Because I have a cold, sir."
"Where did you get your cold, sir?"
"At the North Pole, sir."
"What were you doing there, sir?"
"Shooting polar bear, sir."
"Let me hear you sneeze, sir."
"Kachoo, kachoo, kachoo, sir."

TRADITIONAL

HAND-CLAPPING RHYME

Did you eever iver ever
In your long-legged life,
See a long-legged sailor
Kiss his long-legged wife?

No, I neever niver never
In my long-legged life,
Saw a long-legged sailor
Kiss his long-legged wife!

TRADITIONAL

'TIS MIDNIGHT

'Tis midnight, and the setting sun
   Is slowly rising in the west;
The rapid rivers slowly run,
   The frog is on his downy nest.
The pensive goat and sportive cow,
Hilarious, leap from bough to bough.

AUTHOR UNKNOWN

99

THE PERFECT REACTIONARY

As I was sitting in my chair
I knew the bottom wasn't there,
Nor legs nor back, but *I just sat,*
Ignoring little things like that.

HUGHES MEARNS

THE OLD SUSSEX ROAD

"Do I see a hat in the road?" I said.
I picked up the hat — and I saw a head.
I pulled out a man, who said, "Don't go.
Help pull out my horse. He's down below."

IAN SERRAILLIER

THE PURPLE COW

I never saw a Purple Cow,
   I never hope to see one;
But I can tell you, anyhow,
   I'd rather see than be one.

GELETT BURGESS

AS I WAS STANDING IN THE STREET

As I was standing in the street,
   As quiet as could be,
A great big ugly man came up
   And tied his horse to me.

AUTHOR UNKNOWN

NICHOLAS NED

Nicholas Ned,
   He lost his head,
And put a turnip on instead;
   But then, ah, me!
   He could not see,
So he thought it was night, and he went to bed.

AUTHOR UNKNOWN

ELETELEPHONY

Once there was an elephant,
Who tried to use the telephant—
No! no! I mean an elephone
Who tried to use the telephone—
(Dear me! I am not certain quite
That even now I've got it right.)

Howe'er it was, he got his trunk
Entangled in the telephunk;
The more he tried to get it free,
The louder buzzed the telephee—
(I fear I'd better drop the song
Of elephop and telephong!)

LAURA E. RICHARDS

W

The King sent for his wise men all
　To find a rhyme for W;
When they had thought a good long time
But could not think of a single rhyme,
　"I'm sorry," said he, "to trouble you."

JAMES REEVES

ICE CREAM CHANT

I scream, you scream,
We all scream for ice cream.

TRADITIONAL

FUZZY WUZZY WAS A BEAR

Fuzzy Wuzzy was a bear;
Fuzzy Wuzzy had no hair.
Fuzzy Wuzzy wasn't fuzzy,
Was he?

TRADITIONAL

A B C D GOLDFISH

A B C D goldfish?
L M N O goldfish.
O S A R goldfish.

TRADITIONAL

103

THE OWL AND THE PUSSY-CAT

The Owl and the Pussy-cat went to sea
   In a beautiful pea-green boat:
They took some honey, and plenty of money
   Wrapped up in a five-pound note.
The Owl looked up to the stars above,
   And sang to a small guitar,
"O lovely Pussy, O Pussy, my love,
   What a beautiful Pussy you are,
        You are,
        You are!
   What a beautiful Pussy you are!"

Pussy said to the Owl, "You elegant fowl,
   How charmingly sweet you sing!
Oh! let us be married; too long we have tarried:
   But what shall we do for a ring?"
They sailed away, for a year and a day,
   To the land where the bong-tree grows;
And there in a wood a Piggy-wig stood,
   With a ring at the end of his nose,
        His nose,
        His nose,
   With a ring at the end of his nose.

"Dear Pig, are you willing to sell for one shilling
   Your ring?" Said the Piggy, "I will."
So they took it away, and were married next day
   By the turkey who lives on the hill.
They dinèd on mince and slices of quince,
   Which they ate with a runcible spoon;
And hand in hand, on the edge of the sand,
   They danced by the light of the moon,
        The moon,
        The moon,
   They danced by the light of the moon.

EDWARD LEAR

Riddle Rhymes

Thirty white horses upon a red hill,
Now they tramp, now they champ,
  Now they stand still.

The teeth

        Little Nanny Etticoat
        In a white petticoat,
          And a red nose;
        The longer she stands
        The shorter she grows.

A candle

Two legs sat upon three legs,
With one leg in his lap;
In comes four legs,
And runs away with one leg.
Up jumps two legs,
Catches up three legs,
Throws it after four legs,
And makes him bring back one leg.

*A man (two legs); a stool (three legs);
a leg of mutton (one leg); a dog (four legs)*

        Lives in winter,
        Dies in summer,
        And grows with its roots upward!

An icicle

As I was going to St. Ives
I met a man with seven wives;
Every wife had seven sacks;
Every sack had seven cats;
Every cat had seven kits.
Kits, cats, sacks, and wives—
How many were going to St. Ives?

One (the "I" in the first line)

Old Mother Twitchett had but one eye,
And a long tail which she let fly;
And every time she went through a gap,
A bit of her tail she left in a trap.

A needle and thread

It has a head like a cat, feet like a cat,
A tail like a cat, but it isn't a cat.

A kitten

House full, yard full,
You can't catch a spoonful.

Smoke

107

THE LAZY PEOPLE

Let's write a poem about lazy people
Who lazily laze their lives away;
Let's finish it tomorrow,
I'm much too tired today.

SHEL SILVERSTEIN

THE RAIN IT RAINETH

The rain it raineth on the just
    And also on the unjust fella;
But chiefly on the just, because
    The unjust steals the just's umbrella.

CHARLES BOWEN

FRIENDSHIP

I've discovered a way to stay friends forever—
There's really nothing to it.
I simply tell you what to do
And you do it!

SHEL SILVERSTEIN

GET UP, GET UP

Get up, get up, you lazy-head,
 Get up, you lazy sinner,
We need those sheets for tablecloths,
 It's nearly time for dinner!

AUTHOR UNKNOWN

WILLIE THE POISONER

Willie poisoned Auntie's tea.
Auntie died in agony.
Uncle came and looked quite vexed,
"Really, Will," said he, "what next?"

AUTHOR UNKNOWN

A HORSE AND A FLEA AND
THREE BLIND MICE

A horse and a flea and three blind mice
Sat on a curbstone shooting dice.
The horse he slipped and fell on the flea.
The flea said, "Whoops, there's a horse on me."

AUTHOR UNKNOWN

I EAT MY PEAS WITH HONEY

I eat my peas with honey;
I've done it all my life.
It makes the peas taste funny,
But it keeps them on the knife!

AUTHOR UNKNOWN

DISOBEDIENCE

James James
Morrison Morrison
Weatherby George Dupree
Took great
Care of his Mother,
Though he was only three.
James James
Said to his Mother,
"Mother," he said, said he:
"You must never go down to the end of the town,
    if you don't go down with me."

James James
Morrison's Mother
Put on a golden gown,
James James
Morrison's Mother
Drove to the end of the town.
James James
Morrison's Mother
Said to herself, said she:
"I can get right down to the end of the town and be
    back in time for tea."

King John
Put up a notice,
"LOST or STOLEN or STRAYED!
JAMES JAMES
MORRISON'S MOTHER
SEEMS TO HAVE BEEN MISLAID.
LAST SEEN
WANDERING VAGUELY:
QUITE OF HER OWN ACCORD,
SHE TRIED TO GET DOWN TO THE END
OF THE TOWN—FORTY SHILLINGS
REWARD!"

James James
Morrison Morrison
(Commonly known as Jim)
Told his
Other relations
Not to go blaming *him*.
James James
Said to his Mother,
"Mother," he said, said he:
"You must *never* go down to the end of the town
without consulting me."

James James
Morrison's Mother
Hasn't been heard of since.
King John
Said he was sorry,
So did the Queen and Prince.
King John
(Somebody told me)
Said to a man he knew:
"If people go down to the end of the town, well,
what can *anyone* do?"

(*Now then, very softly*)
J. J.
M. M.
W. G. Du P.
Took great
C/o his M*****
Though he was only 3.
J. J.
Said to his M*****
"M*****," he said, said he:
"You-must-never-go-down-to-the-end-of-the-town-
if-you-don't-go-down-with ME!"

A. A. MILNE

NOT ME

The Slithergadee has crawled out of the sea.
He may catch all the others, but he won't catch me.
No you won't catch me, old Slithergadee,
You may catch all the others, but you wo—

SHEL SILVERSTEIN

OLD MAN WITH A BEARD

There was an Old Man with a beard
Who said, "It is just as I feared!
  Two Owls and a Hen,
  Four Larks and a Wren,
Have all built their nests in my beard!"

EDWARD LEAR

OLD MAN FROM DARJEELING

There was an old man from Darjeeling,
Who boarded a bus bound for Ealing.
    He saw on the door:
    "Please don't spit on the floor,"
So he stood up and spat on the ceiling.

Author Unknown

OLD MAN FROM PERU

There was an old man from Peru
Who dreamed he was eating his shoe.
    In the midst of the night
    He awoke in a fright
And—good grief! it was perfectly true!

Author Unknown

AN EPICURE, DINING AT CREWE

An epicure, dining at Crewe,
Found quite a large mouse in his stew.
  Said the waiter, "Don't shout,
  And wave it about,
Or the rest will be wanting one too!"

AUTHOR UNKNOWN

JABBERWOCKY

'Twas brillig, and the slithy toves
   Did gyre and gimble in the wabe:
All mimsy were the borogoves,
    And the mome raths outgrabe.

"Beware the Jabberwock, my son!
   The jaws that bite, the claws that catch!
Beware the Jubjub bird, and shun
    The frumious Bandersnatch!"

He took his vorpal sword in hand:
   Long time the manxome foe he sought—
So rested he by the Tumtum tree,
    And stood awhile in thought.

And, as in uffish thought he stood,
   The Jabberwock, with eyes of flame,
Came whiffling through the tulgey wood,
     And burbled as it came!

One, two! One, two! And through and through
   The vorpal blade went snicker-snack!
He left it dead, and with its head
     He went galumphing back.

"And hast thou slain the Jabberwock?
   Come to my arms, my beamish boy!
O frabjous day! Callooh! Callay!"
     He chortled in his joy.

'Twas brillig, and the slithy toves
   Did gyre and gimble in the wabe:
All mimsy were the borogoves,
     And the mome raths outgrabe.

LEWIS CARROLL

119

ONE, TWO, THREE—GOUGH!

To make some bread you must have dough,
Isn't that sough?

If the sky is clear all through,
Is the color of it blough?

When is the time to put your hand to the plough?
Nough!

The handle on the pump near the trough
Nearly fell ough.

Bullies sound rough and tough enough,
But you can often call their blough.

EVE MERRIAM

Come Play With Me

Grown-ups don't play, only kids do—right? Wrong! The most creative grown-ups keep on playing, and perhaps poets are the most playful of people—always playing with words.

They remember very well, anyway, what it feels like to be a child at play, and they write poetry about baseball and skateboarding and kite flying and just running a stick along the slats of a picket fence to hear the clatter.

THE PICKETY FENCE

The pickety fence
The pickety fence
Give it a lick it's
The pickety fence
Give it a lick it's
A clickety fence
Give it a lick it's
A lickety fence
Give it a lick
Give it a lick
Give it a lick
With a rickety stick
Pickety
Pickety
Pickety
Pick

DAVID McCORD

EVERY TIME I CLIMB A TREE

Every time I climb a tree
Every time I climb a tree
Every time I climb a tree
I scrape a leg
Or skin a knee
And every time I climb a tree
I find some ants
Or dodge a bee
And get the ants
All over me

And every time I climb a tree
Where have you been?
They say to me
But don't they know that I am free
Every time I climb a tree?
I like it best
To spot a nest
That has an egg
Or maybe three

And then I skin
The other leg
But every time I climb a tree
I see a lot of things to see
Swallows rooftops and TV
And all the fields and farms there be
Every time I climb a tree
Though climbing may be good for ants
It isn't awfully good for pants
But still it's pretty good for me
Every time I climb a tree

DAVID MCCORD

AT THE SEA-SIDE

When I was down beside the sea
A wooden spade they gave to me
   To dig the sandy shore.

My holes were empty like a cup.
In every hole the sea came up,
   Till it could come no more.

ROBERT LOUIS STEVENSON

PLAY

Come play with me said the sun,
come play with me said the earth,
come play with me said the sky.
What shall we play said I?

Let's fly a kite said the sun,
stand on me said the earth,
I'll bring the wind said the sky,
I'll hold the string said I.

FRANK ASCH

THE SWING

How do you like to go up in a swing,
   Up in the air so blue?
Oh, I do think it the pleasantest thing
   Ever a child can do!

Up in the air and over the wall,
   Till I can see so wide,
Rivers and trees and cattle and all
   Over the countryside—

Till I look down on the garden green,
   Down on the roof so brown—
Up in the air I go flying again,
   Up in the air and down!

ROBERT LOUIS STEVENSON

THE LAND OF COUNTERPANE

When I was sick and lay abed,
I had two pillows at my head,
And all my toys beside me lay
To keep me happy all the day.

And sometimes for an hour or so
I watched my leaden soldiers go,
With different uniforms and drills,
Among the bedclothes, through the hills;

And sometimes sent my ships in fleets
All up and down among the sheets;
Or brought my trees and houses out,
And planted cities all about.

I was the giant great and still
That sits upon the pillow-hill,
And sees before him, dale and plain,
The pleasant Land of Counterpane.

ROBERT LOUIS STEVENSON

BLOCK CITY

What are you able to build with your blocks?
Castles and palaces, temples and docks.
Rain may keep raining, and others go roam,
But I can be happy and building at home.

Let the sofa be mountains, the carpet be sea,
There I'll establish a city for me:
A kirk and a mill and a palace beside,
And a harbor as well where my vessels may ride.

Great is the palace with pillar and wall,
A sort of a tower on the top of it all,
And steps coming down in an orderly way
To where my toy vessels lie safe in the bay.

This one is sailing and that one is moored:
Hark to the song of the sailors on board!
And see on the steps of my palace, the kings
Coming and going with presents and things!

ROBERT LOUIS STEVENSON

WHERE GO THE BOATS?

Dark brown is the river,
   Golden is the sand.
It flows along for ever,
   With trees on either hand.

Green leaves a-floating,
   Castles of the foam,
Boats of mine a-boating—
   Where will all come home?

On goes the river
   And out past the mill,
Away down the valley,
   Away down the hill.

Away down the river,
   A hundred miles or more,
Other little children
   Shall bring my boats ashore.

ROBERT LOUIS STEVENSON

NARCISSA

Some of the girls are playing jacks.
Some are playing ball.
But small Narcissa is not playing
Anything at all.

Small Narcissa sits upon
A brick in her back yard
And looks at tiger lilies,
And shakes her pigtails hard.

First she is an ancient queen
In pomp and purple veil.
Soon she is a singing wind.
And, next, a nightingale.

How fine to be Narcissa,
A-changing like all that!
While sitting still, as still, as still
As anyone ever sat!

GWENDOLYN BROOKS

LITTLE JUMPING JOAN

Here am I, little jumping Joan,
    When nobody's with me
    I'm always alone.

MOTHER GOOSE

I CAN FLY

I can fly, of course,
Very low,
Not fast,
Rather slow.
I spread my arms
Like wings,
Lean on the wind,
And my body zings
About.
Nothing showy—
A few loops
And turns—
But for the most
Part,
I just coast.

However,
Since people are prone
To talk about
It,
I generally prefer,
Unless I am alone,
Just to walk about.

FELICE HOLMAN

SUMMER

When it's hot
I take my shoes off,
I take my shirt off,
I take my pants off,
I take my underwear off,
I take my whole body off,
and throw it
in the river.

FRANK ASCH

THE BASE STEALER

Poised between going on and back, pulled
Both ways taut like a tightrope-walker,
Fingertips pointing the opposites,
Now bouncing tiptoe like a dropped ball
Or a kid skipping rope, come on, come on,
Running a scattering of steps sidewise,
How he teeters, skitters, tingles, teases,
Taunts them, hovers like an ecstatic bird,
He's only flirting, crowd him, crowd him,
Delicate, delicate, delicate, delicate — now!

ROBERT FRANCIS

THE SIDEWALK RACER
or
On the Skateboard

Skimming
an asphalt sea
I swerve, I curve, I
sway; I speed to whirring
sound an inch above the
ground; I'm the sailor
and the sail, I'm the
driver and the wheel
I'm the one and only
single engine
human auto
mobile.

LILLIAN MORRISON

HIDE AND SEEK

The trees are tall, but the moon small,
My legs feel rather weak,
For Avis, Mavis and Tom Clarke
Are hiding somewhere in the dark
And it's my turn to seek.

Suppose they lay a trap and play
A trick to frighten me?
Suppose they plan to disappear
And leave me here, half-dead with fear,
Groping from tree to tree?

Alone, alone, all on my own
And then perhaps to find
Not Avis, Mavis and young Tom
But monsters to run shrieking from,
Mad monsters of no kind?

ROBERT GRAVES

When I Went Out to See the Sun

"Let the rain kiss you." Hear the "rain, lap, fold, slap" of water coming down. Watch "snow falling . . . knitting caps up church spires." Listen to the sea as it "breathes in and out upon a shore." Pin the night to the sky "with a million stars."

Don't these images from poems about seasons, weather, sea, earth, and sky seem more real than the weather report with its degree days and windchill factors?

STOPPING BY WOODS ON A SNOWY EVENING

Whose woods these are I think I know.
His house is in the village though;
He will not see me stopping here
To watch his woods fill up with snow.

My little horse must think it queer
To stop without a farmhouse near
Between the woods and frozen lake
The darkest evening of the year.

He gives his harness bells a shake
To ask if there is some mistake.
The only other sound's the sweep
Of easy wind and downy flake.

The woods are lovely, dark and deep.
But I have promises to keep,
And miles to go before I sleep.
And miles to go before I sleep.

ROBERT FROST

SNOWFALL

Snow falling
Snow falling up poles.
Snow falling into holes.
Toeing tight on high wires,
knitting caps up church spires,
dropping hats on hydrants. Now
then watch it balance
on the roof, slide down
the drainpipe, clown up
the fire escape. See
it ape in white lace
drape the black iron
marching fence, gather
into whirls, blow in
the gate, up the walk.
Door, doorstep, windowpane,
colors, shapes lose their name.
Look now before the view
is closed, the trusted clues
you used to know lost
under falling snow,
falling snow,
falling snow.

ARTIS BERNARD

I HEARD A BIRD SING

I heard a bird sing
  In the dark of December
A magical thing
  And sweet to remember.
"We are nearer to Spring
  Than we were in September,"
I heard a bird sing
  In the dark of December.

OLIVER HERFORD

FIRST SIGHT

Lambs that learn to walk in snow
When their bleating clouds the air
Meet a vast unwelcome, know
Nothing but a sunless glare.
Newly stumbling to and fro
All they find, outside the fold,
Is a wretched width of cold.

As they wait beside the ewe,
Her fleeces wetly caked, there lies
Hidden round them, waiting too,
Earth's immeasurable surprise.
They could not grasp it if they knew,
What so soon will wake and grow
Utterly unlike the snow.

PHILIP LARKIN

PIPPA'S SONG

The year's at the spring,
And day's at the morn;
Morning's at seven;
The hillside's dew-pearled;
The lark's on the wing;
The snail's on the thorn;
God's in His heaven—
All's right with the world.

ROBERT BROWNING

WRITTEN IN MARCH

The Cock is crowing,
The stream is flowing,
The small birds twitter,
The lake doth glitter,
The green field sleeps in the sun;
The oldest and youngest
Are at work with the strongest;
The cattle are grazing,
Their heads never raising;
There are forty feeding like one!

Like an army defeated
The snow hath retreated,
And now doth fare ill
On the top of the bare hill;
The ploughboy is whooping—anon—anon:
There's joy in the mountains;
There's life in the fountains;
Small clouds are sailing,
Blue sky prevailing;
The rain is over and gone!

WILLIAM WORDSWORTH

I BENDED UNTO ME

I bended unto me a bough of may,
That I might see and smell:
It bore it in a sort of way,
It bore it very well.
But when I let it backward sway,
Then it were hard to tell
With what a toss, with what a swing,
The dainty thing
Resumed its proper level,
And sent me to the devil.
I know it did—you doubt it?
I turned, and saw them whispering about it.

T. E. BROWN

APRIL RAIN SONG

Let the rain kiss you.
Let the rain beat upon your head with silver liquid drops.
Let the rain sing you a lullaby.

The rain makes still pools on the sidewalk.
The rain makes running pools in the gutter.
The rain plays a little sleep-song on our roof at night—

And I love the rain.

LANGSTON HUGHES

WHEN I WENT OUT

When I went out to see the sun
There wasn't sun or anyone
But there was only sand and sea
And lots of rain that fell on me
And where the rain and river met
The water got completely wet.

KARLA KUSKIN

145

THAT WAS SUMMER

Have you ever smelled summer?
Sure you have.
Remember that time
when you were tired of running
or doing nothing much
and you were hot
and you flopped right down on the ground?
Remember how the warm soil smelled
and the grass?
That was summer.

Remember that time
when the storm blew up quick
and you stood under a ledge
and watched the rain till it stopped
and when it stopped
you walked out again to the sidewalk,
the quiet sidewalk?
Remember how the pavement smelled —
all steamy warm and wet?
That was summer.

Remember that time
when you were trying to climb
higher in the tree
and you didn't know how
and your foot was hurting in the fork
but you were holding tight
to the branch?
Remember how the bark smelled then —
all dusty dry, but nice?
That was summer.

If you try very hard
can you remember that time
when you played outside all day
and you came home for dinner
and had to take a bath right away,
right away?
It took you a long time to pull
your shirt over your head.
Do you remember smelling the sunshine?
That was summer.

MARCI RIDLON

SOUND OF WATER

The sound of water is:
Rain,
Lap,
Fold,
Slap,
Gurgle,
Splash,
Churn,
Crash,
Murmur,
Pour,
Ripple,
Roar,
Plunge,
Drip,
Spout,
Skip,
Sprinkle,
Flow,
Ice,
Snow.

MARY O'NEILL

UNTIL I SAW THE SEA

Until I saw the sea
I did not know
that wind
could wrinkle water so.

I never knew
that sun
could splinter a whole sea of blue.

Nor
did I know before,
a sea breathes in and out
upon a shore.

LILIAN MOORE

THE HORSES OF THE SEA

The horses of the sea
   Rear a foaming crest,
But the horses of the land
   Serve us the best.

The horses of the land
   Munch corn and clover,
While the foaming sea-horses
   Toss and turn over.

CHRISTINA GEORGINA ROSSETTI

THE NIGHT WILL NEVER STAY

The night will never stay,
The night will still go by,
Though with a million stars
You pin it to the sky;
Though you bind it with the blowing wind
And buckle it with the moon,
The night will slip away
Like a sorrow or a tune.

ELEANOR FARJEON

WHO HAS SEEN THE WIND?

Who has seen the wind?
  Neither I nor you:
But when the leaves hang trembling,
  The wind is passing through.

Who has seen the wind?
  Neither you nor I:
But when the trees bow down their heads,
  The wind is passing by.

CHRISTINA GEORGINA ROSSETTI

151

LEAVES

"My green leaves are more beautiful
than your white clouds,"
said the maple to the sky.
"That's a lie," said the sky.
"At sunset my pinks and purples
make me more beautiful than you."
The maple was angry and
for the first time being just green
made it feel blue.
"Let's ask Mother Earth for a favor,"
said the maple to the pine.
"Go ahead," said the pine tree.
"The way I am is just fine with me."
"Mother Earth," said the maple,
"make my leaves more beautiful
than the sky at sunset."
"You will regret that request,"
said Mother Earth.
"No, I will not," said the maple.
"Believe me I can feel it in my sap."
"Then it is done," said Mother Earth.
"Now leave me alone to take my winter nap."

Day by day the leaves of the maple
turned yellow and orange and red.
And the compliments he got
from the animals of the forest
went straight to his head.
Now the sky was jealous
and sent down a breeze
to steal the maple leaves.
"Dance with me," said the sky,
"and fall where you please."
"You are mean," said the maple
and shook its bare branches at the sky.
"Let it be a lesson to you,"
replied the sky.
"There is no one more beautiful than I."

FRANK ASCH

SOMETHING TOLD THE WILD GEESE

Something told the wild geese
   It was time to go.
Though the fields lay golden
   Something whispered, — "Snow."
Leaves were green and stirring,
   Berries luster-glossed,
But beneath warm feathers
   Something cautioned, — "Frost."
All the sagging orchards
   Steamed with amber spice,
But each wild breast stiffened
   At remembered ice.
Something told the wild geese
   It was time to fly, —
Summer sun was on their wings,
   Winter in their cry.

RACHEL FIELD

Celebrate the Time

There are so many ways to think about a holiday. Some poets describe the sounds, sights, and textures of the day as we celebrate it. Reading "Day Before Christmas" by Marchette Chute, one can almost see all the holiday preparations completed and feel how slowly the time is passing for the impatient children.

Other poets write about the meaning of a day. Jack Prelutsky does this when he tells the story of "The First Thanksgiving" in sure, simple verse.

For other poets, the holiday seems to set them thinking, and they follow their thoughts where they lead. Myra Cohn Livingston, for instance, finds herself marveling in "12 October" that Columbus could have discovered that the earth is round when it still seems so flat to her today. And Rosemary Carr and Stephen Vincent Benét imagine Abe Lincoln's mother, Nancy Hanks, coming back as a ghost in a poem that is moving to read on that President's birthday.

HAPPY NEW YEAR, ANYWAY

January first isn't New Year's.
Everyone knows that.
The real new year is in September
when school starts.
January comes in the middle of the year,
when the edges of your notebook are all worn
and those new pencils with your name in gold
have been broken or borrowed or lost.
And your mother starts looking at your shoes
and saying, "Are those getting too tight for you?"
Everything's old by January.
The teacher has long since stopped
playing games to learn your names
and asking how your summer was.
And you're right in the middle,
smack in the middle of the hardest math.
There's nothing new about January.
But your parents don't know that,
with their party horns and midnight kisses.
And they have the calendar on their side.
So Happy New Year, anyway.
You might as well pretend.

JOANNA COLE

SONG

Tomorrow is Saint Valentine's day,
  All in the morning betime,
And I a maid at your window,
  To be your Valentine.

WILLIAM SHAKESPEARE

158

VALENTINE

Chipmunks jump, and
Greensnakes slither.
Rather burst than
Not be with her.

Bluebirds fight, but
Bears are stronger.
We've got fifty
Years or longer.

Hoptoads hop, but
Hogs are fatter.
Nothing else but
Us can matter.

DONALD HALL

JENNY KISS'D ME

Jenny kiss'd me when we met,
    Jumping from the chair she sat in;
Time, you thief, who love to get
    Sweets into your list, put that in!
Say I'm weary, say I'm sad,
    Say that health and wealth have miss'd me,
Say I'm growing old, but add,
    Jenny kiss'd me.

LEIGH HUNT

PHOEBE IN A ROSEBUSH

Phoebe in a rosebush
Phoebe in a tree
There's many a Phoebe in the world
But you're the one for me

CLYDE WATSON

NANCY HANKS
1784–1818

If Nancy Hanks
Came back as a ghost,
Seeking news
Of what she loved most,
She'd ask first
"Where's my son?
What's happened to Abe?
What's he done?

"Poor little Abe,
Left all alone
Except for Tom,
Who's a rolling stone;
He was only nine
The year I died.
I remember still
How hard he cried.

"Scraping along
In a little shack,
With hardly a shirt
To cover his back,
And a prairie wind
To blow him down,
Or pinching times
If he went to town.

"You wouldn't know
About my son?
Did he grow tall?
Did he have fun?
Did he learn to read?
Did he get to town?
Do you know his name?
Did he get on?"

ROSEMARY CARR AND
STEPHEN VINCENT BENÉT

WHICH WASHINGTON?

There are many Washingtons:
Which one do you like best?
The rich man with his powdered wig
And silk brocaded vest?

The sportsman from Virginia
Riding with his hounds,
Sounding a silver trumpet
On the green replendent grounds?

The President with his tricorn hat
And polished leather boots,
With scarlet capes and ruffled shirts
And fine brass-buttoned suits?

Or the patchwork man with ragged feet,
Freezing at Valley Forge,
Richer in courage than all of them —
Though all of them were George.

EVE MERRIAM

ON MOTHER'S DAY

On Mother's Day we got up first
so full of plans we almost burst.

We started breakfast right away
as our surprise for Mother's Day.

We picked some flowers, then hurried back
to make the coffee—rather black.

We wrapped our gifts and wrote a card
and boiled the eggs—a little hard.

And then we sang a serenade,
which burned the toast, I am afraid.

But Mother said, amidst our cheers,
"Oh, what a big surprise, my dears,
I've not had such a treat in years."
And she was smiling to her ears!

AILEEN FISHER

163

FATHER

Carrying my world
Your head tops ceilings.
Your shoulders split door frames.
Your back holds up walls.

You are bigger than all sounds of laughter,
of weeping,
Your hand in mine keeps us straight ahead.

MYRA COHN LIVINGSTON

FIREWORKS

First
A far thud,
Then the rocket
Climbs the air,
A dull red flare,
To hang, a moment,
Invisible, before
Its shut black shell cracks
And claps against the ears,
Breaks and billows into bloom,
Spilling down clear green sparks, gold spears,
Silent sliding silver waterfalls and stars.

VALERIE WORTH

12 OCTOBER

From where I stand now
    the world is flat,
    flat out flat,
    no end to that.

    Where my eyes go the land moves out.

    How is it then
    five hundred years ago (about)
    Columbus found
    that far beyond the flat on flat
    the world was round?

MYRA COHN LIVINGSTON

IT'S HALLOWEEN

It's Halloween! It's Halloween!
The moon is full and bright
And we shall see what can't be seen
On any other night:

Skeletons and ghosts and ghouls,
Grinning goblins fighting duels,
Werewolves rising from their tombs,
Witches on their magic brooms.

In masks and gowns
  we haunt the street
And knock on doors
  for trick or treat.

Tonight we are
  the king and queen,
For oh tonight
  it's Halloween!

JACK PRELUTSKY

LISTEN!

Listen!
Listen to the witch!

grinch grinch grunch

chip-chop crunch

grickle

grackle

grooble

grobble

munch

munch

munch

Whatever in the world
is she having for lunch?

168   LILIAN MOORE

BEDTIME STORIES

"Tell me a story,"
Says Witch's Child.

"About the Beast
So fierce and wild.

About a Ghost
That shrieks and groans.

A Skeleton
That rattles bones.

About a Monster
Crawly-creepy.

Something nice
To make me sleepy."

LILIAN MOORE

SKELETON PARADE

The skeletons are out tonight,
They march about the street
With bony bodies, bony heads
And bony hands and feet.

Bony bony bony bones
With nothing in between,
Up and down and all around
They march on Halloween.

JACK PRELUTSKY

WITCHES' SPELLS

*(The first spell changes a person into a frog.
The second spell turns him back again.)*

1x

Turn to right, turn to left,
Turn together newt and eft.
Slimy marsh and muddy bog,
Turn from person into frog.

2x

Turn to left, turn to right,
Fading day must turn to night.
Caldron bubble and fire burn,
To your natural shape return!

MADELEINE EDMONDSON

THINGS THAT GO BUMP IN THE NIGHT

From ghoulies and ghosties,
Long-leggity beasties,
And things that go *bump* in the night,
Good Lord deliver us.

OLD SPELL

THE DARK HOUSE

In a dark, dark wood, there was a dark, dark house,
And in that dark, dark house, there was a dark, dark room,
And in that dark, dark room, there was a dark, dark cupboard,
And in that dark, dark cupboard, there was a dark, dark shelf,
And in that dark, dark shelf, there was a dark, dark box,
And in that dark, dark box, there was a GHOST!

AUTHOR UNKNOWN

THE GOBLIN

A goblin lives in *our* house, in *our* house, in *our*
        house,
A goblin lives in *our* house all the year round.
He bumps
And he jumps
And he thumps
And he stumps
He knocks
And he rocks
And he rattles at the locks.
A goblin lives in *our* house, in *our* house, in *our*
        house,
A goblin lives in *our* house all the year round.

ROSE FYLEMAN

172

THE FIRST THANKSGIVING

When the Pilgrims
first gathered together to share
with their Indian friends
in the mild autumn air,
they lifted their voices
in jubilant praise
for the bread on the table,
the berries and maize,
for field and for forest,
for turkey and deer,
for the bountiful crops
they were blessed with that year.
They were thankful for these
as they feasted away,
and as they were thankful,
we're thankful today.

JACK PRELUTSKY

THANKSGIVING DAY

Over the river and through the wood,
　To grandfather's house we go;
　　The horse knows the way
　　To carry the sleigh
　Through the white and drifted snow.

Over the river and through the wood—
　Oh, how the wind does blow!
　　It stings the toes
　　And bites the nose,
　As over the ground we go.

Over the river and through the wood,
　To have a first-rate play.
　　Hear the bells ring,
　　"Ting-a-ling-ding!"
　Hurrah for Thanksgiving Day!

Over the river and through the wood
　Trot fast, my dapple-gray!
　　Spring over the ground,
　　Like a hunting-hound!
　For this is Thanksgiving Day.

Over the river and through the wood,
　And straight through the barnyard gate.
　　We seem to go
　　Extremely slow,—
　It is so hard to wait!

Over the river and through the wood—
　Now grandmother's cap I spy!
　　Hurrah for the fun!
　　Is the pudding done?
　Hurrah for the pumpkin-pie!

Lydia Maria Child

LIGHT ANOTHER CANDLE

Let all the family gather,
bring your friends along,
light another candle,
sing another song.

It's Hanukkah, Hanukkah,
we make the candles glow
to celebrate a victory
two thousand years ago.

When ancient Jewish heroes
known as Maccabees
battled for the right
to worship as they pleased.

Come, light another candle,
make the *dreidl* spin,
sing yet another song, *hoi!*
chirry, birry, bin.
MIRIAM CHAIKIN

LITTLE TREE

little tree
little silent Christmas tree
you are so little
you are more like a flower

who found you in the green forest
and were you very sorry to come away?
see   i will comfort you
because you smell so sweetly

i will kiss your cool bark
and hug you safe and tight
just as your mother would,
only don't be afraid

look   the spangles
that sleep all the year in a dark box
dreaming of being taken out and allowed to shine,
the balls the chains red and gold the fluffy threads,

put up your little arms
and i'll give them all to you to hold
every finger shall have its ring
and there won't be a single place dark or unhappy

then when you're quite dressed
you'll stand in the window for everyone to see
and how they'll stare!
oh but you'll be very proud

and my little sister and i will take hands
and looking up at our beautiful tree
we'll dance and sing
"Noel Noel"

E. E. CUMMINGS

CHRISTMAS IS A-COMING

Christmas is a-coming,
The goose is getting fat,
Please to put a penny
In an old man's hat.
If you haven't got a penny,
A ha'penny will do.
If you haven't got a ha'penny,
God bless you!

ENGLISH NURSERY RHYME

DAY BEFORE CHRISTMAS

We have been helping with the cake
    And licking out the pan,
And wrapping up our packages
    As neatly as we can.
And we have hung our stockings up
    Beside the open grate.
And now there's nothing more to do
    Except
        to
            wait!

MARCHETTE CHUTE

A VISIT FROM ST. NICHOLAS

'Twas the night before Christmas, when all through the
  house
Not a creature was stirring, not even a mouse;
The stockings were hung by the chimney with care,
In hopes that St. Nicholas soon would be there.
The children were nestled all snug in their beds,
While visions of sugar-plums danced in their heads;
And mamma in her 'kerchief, and I in my cap,
Had just settled our brains for a long winter's nap,
When out on the lawn there arose such a clatter,
I sprang from my bed to see what was the matter.
Away to the window I flew like a flash,
Tore open the shutters and threw up the sash.
The moon on the breast of the new-fallen snow
Gave the luster of midday to objects below,
When, what to my wondering eyes should appear,
But a miniature sleigh, and eight tiny reindeer,
With a little old driver, so lively and quick,
I knew in a moment it must be St. Nick.
More rapid than eagles his coursers they came,
And he whistled, and shouted, and called them by name:
"Now, Dasher! now, Dancer! now, Prancer and Vixen!
On, Comet! on, Cupid! on, Donder and Blitzen!
To the top of the porch! to the top of the wall!
Now dash away! dash away! dash away all!"
As dry leaves that before the wild hurricane fly,
When they meet with an obstacle, mount to the sky,
So up to the housetop the coursers they flew,
With the sleigh full of toys, and St. Nicholas, too.
And then, in a twinkling, I heard on the roof
The prancing and pawing of each little hoof.
As I drew in my head, and was turning around,
Down the chimney St. Nicholas came with a bound.
He was dressed all in fur, from his head to his foot,
And his clothes were all covered with ashes and soot;
A bundle of toys he had flung on his back,
And he looked like a peddler just opening his pack.

His eyes—how they twinkled! his dimples how merry!
His cheeks were like roses, his nose like a cherry!
His droll little mouth was drawn up like a bow,
And the beard on his chin was as white as the snow;
The stump of a pipe he held tight in his teeth,
And the smoke it encircled his head like a wreath;
He had a broad face and a little round belly
That shook, when he laughed, like a bowlful of jelly.
He was chubby and plump, a right jolly old elf,
And I laughed when I saw him, in spite of myself;
A wink of his eye and a twist of his head,
Soon gave me to know I had nothing to dread;
He spoke not a word, but went straight to his work,
And filled all the stockings; then turned with a jerk,
And laying his finger aside of his nose
And giving a nod, up the chimney he rose;
He sprang to his sleigh, to his team gave a whistle,
And away they all flew like the down of a thistle.
But I heard him exclaim, ere he drove out of sight,
"Happy Christmas to all, and to all a good night."

CLEMENT CLARKE MOORE

I HEARD THE BELLS ON CHRISTMAS DAY

I heard the bells on Christmas Day
Their old, familiar carols play,
  And wild and sweet
  The words repeat
Of peace on earth, good-will to men!

HENRY WADSWORTH LONGFELLOW

A Different Way of Seeing

Many poems make us realize that if we can see the world with new eyes, even ordinary things become exciting.

Ocean waves *do* look as if they are sprawling with "arms outstretched" and "foam fingers reaching," as Lillian Morrison says in her poem "Surf." And a steam shovel *can* seem exactly as Charles Malam sees it: a dinosaur with "jaws... dripping with a load of earth and grass that it had cropped." Even a color we see every day holds new possibilities in a poem. Mary O'Neill enriches a color for us in "What Is Black?" as she imagines things that are black from "patent leather shoes" to "the print in the news" and the "darkest cloud in a thunderstorm."

HOUSES

Houses are faces
(haven't you found?)
with their hats in the air,
and their necks in the ground.

Windows are noses,
windows are eyes,
and doors are the mouths
of a suitable size.

And a porch—or the place
where porches begin—
is just like a mustache
shading the chin.

AILEEN FISHER

THE MOON'S THE NORTH WIND'S COOKY

The Moon's the North Wind's cooky.
He bites it, day by day,
Until there's but a rim of scraps
That crumble all away.

The South Wind is a baker.
He kneads clouds in his den,
And bakes a crisp new moon *that... greedy*
North... Wind... eats... again!

VACHEL LINDSAY

THE GARDEN HOSE

In the grey evening
I see a long green serpent
With its tail in the dahlias.

It lies in loops across the grass
And drinks softly at the faucet.

I can hear it swallow.

BEATRICE JANOSCO

CONVERSATION

An umbrella
And a raincoat
Are walking and talking together.

BUSON

STEAM SHOVEL

The dinosaurs are not all dead.
I saw one raise its iron head
To watch me walking down the road
Beyond our house today.
Its jaws were dripping with a load
Of earth and grass that it had cropped.
It must have heard me where I stopped,
Snorted white steam my way,
And stretched its long neck out to see,
And chewed, and grinned quite amiably.

CHARLES MALAM

ABOUT AN EXCAVATION

About an excavation
a flock of bright red lanterns
has settled.

CHARLES REZNIKOFF

THE STRANGER IN THE PUMPKIN

The stranger in the pumpkin said:
"It's all dark inside your head.
What a dullard you must be!
Without light how can you see?
Don't you know that heads should shine
From deep inside themselves—like mine?
Well, don't stand there in a pout
With that dark dome sticking out—
It makes me sick to look at it!
Go and get your candle lit!"

JOHN CIARDI

CHAIRS

Chairs
Seem
To
Sit
Down
On
Themselves, almost as if
They were people,
Some fat, some thin;
Settled comfortably
On their own seats,
Some even stretch out their arms
To
Rest.

VALERIE WORTH

THE TAPE

Poor song,
    going around in your cassette
    over and over again, repeating
    the same old tune,
    can you breathe in there?

Come, song,
    going around in your cassette
    over and over again, break out!
    Let me play you
    fresh on my guitar!

MYRA COHN LIVINGSTON

SURF

Waves want
to be wheels.
They jump for it
and fail
fall flat
like pole vaulters
and sprawl
arms outstretched
foam fingers
reaching.

LILLIAN MORRISON

WAKING FROM A NAP ON THE BEACH

Sounds like big
rashers of bacon frying.
I look up from where I'm lying
expecting to see stripes

red and white. My eyes drop shut,
stunned by the sun.
Now the foam is flame, the long
troughs charcoal, but

still it chuckles and sizzles, it
burns and burns, it never gets done.
The sea is that
fat.

MAY SWENSON

WHAT IS BLACK?

Black is the night
When there isn't a star
And you can't tell by looking
Where you are.
Black is a pail of paving tar.
Black is jet
And things you'd like to forget.
Black is a smokestack
Black is a cat,
A leopard, a raven,
A high silk hat.
The sound of black is
"Boom! Boom! Boom!"
Echoing in
An empty room.
Black is kind—
It covers up
The run-down street,
The broken cup.
Black is charcoal
And patio grill,
The soot spots on
The window sill.
Black is a feeling
Hard to explain
Like suffering but
Without the pain.
Black is licorice
And patent leather shoes
Black is the print
In the news.
Black is beauty
In its deepest form,
The darkest cloud
In a thunderstorm.
Think of what starlight
And lamplight would lack
Diamonds and fireflies
If they couldn't lean against
Black....

MARY O'NEILL

SUNFLAKES

If sunlight fell like snowflakes,
gleaming yellow and so bright,
we could build a sunman,
we could have a sunball fight,
we could watch the sunflakes
drifting in the sky.
We could go sleighing
in the middle of July
through sundrifts and sunbanks,
we could ride a sunmobile,
and we could touch sunflakes—
I wonder how they'd feel.

FRANK ASCH

ROCKS

Big rocks into pebbles,
pebbles into sand.
I really hold a million million rocks here in my hand.

FLORENCE PARRY HEIDE

CAR WASH

Car,
    I give you over to
    the broad flapping fingers of a
    mechanical genie,
    squeezing soap on your head,
    wooshing wax in your eyes,
    blowing air on your sides,
    brushing your bottom,
    guiding you through a white house
    and out again, on roaring tracks,
    to a little man in orange,
    wiping off your face.

Car,
    what a surprise!
    how good to see you again
    shining, gleaming.

MYRA COHN LIVINGSTON

SOUTHBOUND ON THE FREEWAY

A tourist came in from Orbitville,
parked in the air, and said:

The creatures of this star
are made of metal and glass.

Through the transparent parts
you can see their guts.

Their feet are round and roll
on diagrams or long

measuring tapes, dark
with white lines.

They have four eyes.
The two in back are red.

Sometimes you can see a five-eyed
one, with a red eye turning

on the top of his head.
He must be special—

the others respect him
and go slow

when he passes, winding
among them from behind.

They all hiss as they glide,
like inches, down the marked

tapes. Those soft shapes,
shadowy inside

the hard bodies—are they
their guts or their brains?

MAY SWENSON

Inside Myself

Often poems are about thoughts and feelings most of us are afraid to admit or don't have words to express. Sometimes when I read a poem like this, I become very peaceful inside—even if the poem is not about happy feelings—because I think, "Yes, I've felt that way too."

I know what it's like to be numb when something sad happens and only cry later, as Freya Littledale describes in her poem "When My Dog Died." I have often felt the wish to be like the flowers in Valerie Worth's "Zinnias" that seem always strong and neat and never wilt. And I know the big, joyful feeling that makes me want to say, with Edna St. Vincent Millay, "I will be the gladdest thing under the sun! I will touch a hundred flowers and not pick one."

AT ANNIKA'S PLACE

At home at Annika's place
they talk to you
like you were big
"What do you think?"
"What's the best way, do you think?"
"What do you think we should do?"
And then:
"Really.
Do you mean it?"
"Maybe so."
"Well, you're really right about that!"
Or:
"No-o-ow, I wonder really
if that's right ..."

I wish it was like Annika's place
at our place.

Siv Widerberg,
Translated by Verne Moberg

BEST?

It's best to be best
It's worst to be worst
Mama, Papa, Teacher
and my friends are the ones who decide
who's the best.

They say:
> You're the greatest
> I like you better than anybody
> 'Atta girl
> Get right in there and show 'em your stuff!
> You did just fine
> Now, *you* can do better than *that*
> Well, you didn't win a gold star...
> You can't jump rope
> You can't jump rope
> Who wins the ribbon
> Who wins the blue ribbon
> Oh, you only won a white ribbon...
> Let's have a contest so it'll be more fun

It's best to be best

right?

SIV WIDERBERG,
TRANSLATED BY VERNE MOBERG

WHERE HAVE YOU BEEN DEAR?

Where
Have you been dear?
What
Have you seen dear?
What
Did you do there?
Who
Went with you there?
Tell me
What's new dear?
What's
New with you dear?
Where
Will you go next?
What
Will you do?

"I do this and I do that.
I go here and I go there.
At times I like to be alone.
There are some thoughts that are my own
I do not wish to share."

KARLA KUSKIN

201

THE QUESTION

People always say to me
"What do you think you'd like to be
When you grow up?"
And I say "Why,
I think I'd like to be the sky
Or be a plane or train or mouse
Or maybe be a haunted house
Or something furry, rough and wild...
Or maybe I will stay a child."

KARLA KUSKIN

IN THE LIBRARY

You're right:
I am too old for THIS.
But I like pictures in my book,
And lots of color, easy words—
You needn't give me such a look!
You're wrong:
I am too young for THAT.
The words are long, the type's too small.
I don't find any pictures there—
I'd never get through that at all!

MICHAEL PATRICK HEARN

EVICTION

What I remember about that day
is boxes stacked across the walk
and couch springs curling through the air
and drawers and tables balanced on the curb
and us, hollering,
leaping up and around
happy to have a playground;

nothing about the empty rooms
nothing about the emptied family.

LUCILLE CLIFTON

ZINNIAS

Zinnias, stout and stiff,
Stand no nonsense: their colors
Stare, their leaves
Grow straight out, their petals
Jut like clipped cardboard,
Round, in neat flat rings.

Even cut and bunched,
Arranged to please us
In the house, in water, they
Will hardly wilt — I know
Someone like zinnias; I wish
I were like zinnias.

VALERIE WORTH

INCIDENT

Once riding in Old Baltimore,
Heart filled, head filled with glee,
I saw a Baltimorean
Staring straight at me.

Now I was eight and very small,
And he was no whit bigger
And so I smiled, but he
Stuck out his tongue and called me nigger.

I saw the whole of Baltimore
From May until November.
Of all the things that happened there—
That's all that I remember.

COUNTEE CULLEN

LISTENING TO GROWNUPS QUARRELING

standing in the hall against the
wall with my little brother, blown
like leaves against the wall by their
voices, my head like a pingpong ball
between the paddles of their anger:
I knew what it meant
to tremble like a leaf.

Cold with their wrath, I heard
the claws of the rain
pounce. Floods
poured through the city,
skies clapped over me,
and I was shaken, shaken
like a mouse
between their jaws.

RUTH WHITMAN

POEM

I loved my friend.
He went away from me.
There's nothing more to say.
The poem ends,
Soft as it began—
I loved my friend.

LANGSTON HUGHES

WHEN MY DOG DIED

When my dog died,
I didn't cry.
I didn't even speak—
not one word.
Then I found his collar
in the closet.
It was made of thick red leather
with a brass buckle.
I held it in my hands
and then I cried
and made his collar wet.

FREYA LITTLEDALE

CRYING

Crying only a little bit
is no use. You must cry
until your pillow is soaked!
Then you can get up and laugh.
Then you can jump in the shower
and splash-splash-splash!
Then you can throw open your window
and, "Ha ha! ha ha!"
And if people say, "Hey,
what's going on up there?"
"Ha ha!" sing back, "Happiness
was hiding in the last tear!
I wept it! Ha ha!"

GALWAY KINNELL

JIGSAW PUZZLE

My beautiful picture of pirates and treasure
Is spoiled, and almost I don't want to start
To put it together; I've lost all the pleasure
I used to find in it: there's one missing part.

I know there's one missing — they lost it, the others,
The last time they played with my puzzle — and maybe
There's more than one missing: along with the brothers
And sisters who borrow my toys there's the baby.

There's a hole in the ship or the sea that it sails on,
And I said to my father, "Well, what shall I do?
It isn't the same now that some of it's gone."
He said, "Put it together; the world's like that too."

RUSSELL HOBAN

A RIDDLE

Once when I was very scared
I met a man who knew.
"How did you know?"
I said to him.
He answered, "I am, too."

Then he said something,
for me too it was true,
"But I'm not scared now
because of you."

CHARLOTTE ZOLOTOW

210

A STORY THAT COULD BE TRUE

If you were exchanged in the cradle and
your real mother died
without ever telling the story
then no one knows your name,
and somewhere in the world
your father is lost and needs you
but you are far away.

He can never find
how true you are, how ready.
When the great wind comes
and the robberies of the rain
you stand on the corner shivering.
The people who go by—
you wonder at their calm.

They miss the whisper that runs
any day in your mind,
"Who are you really, wanderer?"—
and the answer you have to give
no matter how dark and cold
the world around you is:
"Maybe I'm a king."

WILLIAM STAFFORD

ONCE

Once I liked pablum
Once I couldn't find the way to Tommy's house
Once I didn't know how to skate
Once I thought that my mama
was The Only Mama
though other people had mamas too
Once
when I was little, smaller, littler

SIV WIDERBERG
TRANSLATED BY VERNE MOBERG

AFTERNOON ON A HILL

I will be the gladdest thing
    Under the sun!
I will touch a hundred flowers
    And not pick one.

I will look at cliffs and clouds
    With quiet eyes,
Watch the wind bow down the grass,
    And the grass rise.

And when lights begin to show
    Up from the town,
I will mark which must be mine,
    And then start down!

EDNA ST. VINCENT MILLAY

BLESSÈD LORD,
WHAT IT IS TO BE YOUNG

Blessèd Lord, what it is to be young:
To be of, to be for, be among—
   Be enchanted, enthralled,
   Be the caller, the called,
The singer, the song, and the sung.

DAVID McCORD

THE SUN

I told the sun that I was glad,
   I'm sure I don't know why;
Somehow the pleasant way he had
   Of shining in the sky,
Just put a notion in my head
   That wouldn't it be fun
If, walking on the hill, I said
   "I'm happy" to the sun.

JOHN DRINKWATER

THIS IS MY ROCK

This is my rock
And here I run
To steal the secret of the sun;

This is my rock
And here come I
Before the night has swept the sky;

This is my rock,
This is the place
I meet the evening face to face.

David McCord

Title Index

A B C D Goldfish, 103
About an Excavation, 187
Adventures of Isabel, *from*, 90
Afternoon on a Hill, 212
Animal Fair, 63
April Rain Song, 145
As I Was Standing in the Street, 101
At Annika's Place, 199
At the Seaside, 125
At the Zoo, 64

Baby's Drinking Song, 39
Bad and Good, 89
Base Stealer, The, 134
Bats, 74
Bedtime Stories, 169
Best?, 200
Bird, *from* A, 76
Blessed Lord, What It Is to Be Young, 213
Block City, 129

Car Wash, 195
Catalogue, *from*, 68
Catherine, 58
Cat in the Snow, 69
Chairs, 189
Christmas Is A-coming, 178
City Mouse and the Garden Mouse, The, 25
Conversation, 187
Cow, The, 83
Cows, 84
Crickets, 72
Crying, 209
Cupboard, The, 38

Daffadowndilly, 29

Dancing Bear, The, 82
Dark House, The, 172
Day Before Christmas, 178
Dilly Dilly Piccalilli, 36
Dinosaurs, 86
Disobedience, 110
Do the Baby Cake-walk, 19
Down! Down!, 31
Duck, 78
Duck's Ditty, 80

Eagle, The, 77
Eel, The, 89
Eletelephony, 102
Epicure, Dining at Crewe, An, 117
Epigram Engraved on the Collar of a Dog, 65
Every Time I Climb a Tree, 124
Eviction, 203

Father, 164
Fernando, 56
Firefly, 73
Fireworks, 165
First Sight, 142
First Thanksgiving, The, 173
Friendship, 108
Frog, The, 71
Frog, The, 96
Fuzzy Wuzzy Was a Bear, 103

Galoshes, 28
Garden Hose, The, 186
Get Up, Get Up, 109
Glowworm, 72
Goblin, The, 172

Hand-clapping Rhyme, 98
Happy New Year, Anyway, 157
Harvey Always Wins, 57
Hide and Seek, 136
Hippopotamus, 95
Holding Hands, 81

Hoppity, 19
Horse, and a Flea and Three Blind Mice, A, 109
Horses of the Sea, The, 150
House of the Mouse, The, 24
Houses, 185
Hug o' War, 60
Husbands and Wives, 51

I Bended unto Me, 144
I Can Fly, 132
Ice Cream Chant, 103
I Eat My Peas with Honey, 109
If All the World Were Paper, 36
I Heard a Bird Sing, 141
I Heard the Bells on Christmas Day, 182
Incident, 205
In the Library, 203
I Saw a Ship A-sailing, 37
I See the Moon, 33
It's Halloween, 167

Jabberwocky, 118
Jenny Kiss'd Me, 160
Jigsaw Puzzle, 210
Jump-rope Rhyme, 98

Kindness to Animals, 67

Land of Counterpane, The, 128
Last Cry of the Damp Fly, The, 96
Lazy People, The, 108
Leaves, 152
Light Another Candle, 175
Listen!, 168
Listening, 69
Listening to Grownups Quarreling, 206
Little, 52
Little Birds, The, 76
Little Black Bug, 23
Little Elf, The, 40
Little Jumping Joan, 131
Little Tree, 177

Little Turtle, The, 22

Mice, 70
Miss Bitter, 92
Miss T., 59
Mr. 'Gator, 93
Mrs. Peck-Pigeon, 78
Mitten Song, The, 27
Mix a Pancake, 39
Moochie, 52
Moon's the North Wind's Cooky, The, 186
More It Snows, The, 26
Mother to Son, 50
Mud, 30
My Sister Laura, 53

Nancy Hanks 1784–1818, 161
Narcissa, 131
Nicholas Ned, 101
Night Will Never Stay, The, 150
Not Me, 114

Old Man from Darjeeling, 115
Old Man from Peru, 115
Old Man with a Beard, 114
Old Sussex Road, The, 100
Old Women, The, 24
On Buying a Dog, 66
Once, 212
One, Two, Three — Gough!, 120
One-upmanship, 55
On Mother's Day, 163
On This Day, 31
Owl and the Pussy-cat, 104

Perfect Reactionary, 100
Phoebe in a Rosebush, 160
Pickety Fence, The, 123
Pippa's Song, 143
Play, 126
Poem, 207
Purple Cow, The, 101

Question, The, 202

Rain, 29
Rain It Raineth, The, 108
Riddle, A, 210
Riddle Rhymes, 106, 107
Rock, Rock, Sleep, My Baby, 44
Rocks, 194

Sidewalk Racer, The, or, On the Skateboard, 135
Skeleton Parade, 170
Snowfall, 140
Soft-boiled Egg, 89
Some People, 47
Something Told the Wild Geese, 154
Song, 158
Song of the Train, 34
Sound of Water, 148
Southbound on the Freeway, 196
Star, The, 32
Steam Shovel, 187
Stopping by Woods on a Snowy Evening, 139
Story That Could Be True, A, 211
Stranger in the Pumpkin, The, 188
Summer, 133
Sun, The, 213
Sunflakes, 194
Surf, 191
Swing, The, 127

Tape, The, 190
Teddy Bear, Teddy Bear, 33
Thanksgiving Day, 174
That Was Summer, 146
There *Once* Was a Puffin, 20
Things That Go Bump in the Night, 171
This Is My Rock, 214
This Little House Is Sugar, 38
Tickle Rhyme, The, 73
Tip-toe Tail, 94
Tired Tim, 47
'Tis Midnight, 99

Toucan, The, 79
Tree Toad, 97
12 October, 166
Two in Bed, 53

Until I Saw the Sea, 149

Valentine, 159
Visit from St. Nicholas, A, 179

W, 102
Waking from a Nap on the Beach, 191
What Is Black?, 193
When Father Carves the Duck, 48
When I Went Out, 145
When My Dog Died, 208
When Young Melissa Sweeps, 54
Where Go the Boats?, 130
Where Have You Been Dear?, 201
Which Washington?, 162
Who Has Seen the Wind, 151
Willie the Poisoner, 109
Wishing Poem, 32
Witches' Spells, 171
Wren, The, 76
Written in March, 143
Wynken, Blynken, and Nod, 42

Zinnias, 204

Author Index

Aldis, Dorothy, 52
Allen, Marie Louise, 27
Asch, Frank, 126, 133, 152, 194

Bacmeister, Rhoda, 28
Bangs, John Kendrick, 40
Belloc, Hilaire, 71
Benét, Stephen Vincent, 161
Bernard, Artis, 140
Bodecker, N. M. 92, 93
Bowen, Charles, 108
Boyden, Polly Chase, 30
Brooks, Gwendolyn, 131
Brown, Margaret Wise, 23
Brown, T. E., 144
Browning, Robert, 143
Burgess, Gelett, 101
Buson, 187

Carr, Rosemary, 161
Carroll, Lewis, 118
Chaikin, Miriam, 55, 175
Child, Lydia Maria, 174
Chute, Marchette, 178
Ciardi, John, 188
Clifton, Lucille, 203
Cole, Joanna, 95, 157
Cullen, Countee, 205
cummings, e. e., 177

De la Mare, Walter, 38, 47, 59
Dickinson, Emily, 76
Drinkwater, John, 213

Edmondson, Madeleine, 171

Farjeon, Eleanor, 31, 78, 150

Field, Eugene, 42
Field, Rachel, 47, 82, 154
Fisher, Aileen, 69, 163, 185
Francis, Robert, 134
Frost, Robert, 139
Fyleman, Rose, 70, 172

Goffstein, M. B., 31
Grahame, Kenneth, 80
Graves, Robert, 136
Greenfield, Eloise, 52

Hall, Donald, 159
Hearn, Michael Patrick, 203
Heide, Florence Parry, 194
Herford, Oliver, 141
Hershenson, Miriam, 51
Hoban, Russell, 89, 210
Holman, Felice, 132
Hughes, Langston, 38, 50, 145, 207
Hunt, Leigh, 160

Issa, 76

Jaques, Florence Page, 20
Janosco, Beatrice, 186
Jarrell, Randall, 74
Johnson, Pyke, Jr., 79

Kinnell, Galway, 209
Kirkup, James, 39
Klauber, Edgar, 66
Kuskin, Karla, 58, 145, 201, 202

Larkin, Philip, 142
Lear, Edward, 104, 114
Lee, Dennis, 96
Lindsay, Vachel, 22, 186
Link, Lenore M., 81
Littledale, Freya, 208
Livingston, Myra Cohn, 164, 166, 190, 195
Longfellow, Henry Wadsworth, 182

McCord, David, 34, 72, 123, 124, 213, 214
Malam, Charles, 187
Mearns, Hughes, 100
Merriam, Eve, 120, 162
Millay, Edna St. Vincent, 212
Milligan, Spike, 53
Milne, A. A., 19, 26, 110
Mitchell, Lucy Sprague, 24
Moore, Clement Clarke, 179
Moore, Lilian, 149, 168, 169
Moore, Rosalie, 68
Morrison, Lillian, 135, 191
Mother Goose, 29, 37, 131

Nash, Ogden, 89, 90

O'Neill, Mary, 148, 193

Pope, Alexander, 65
Potter, Beatrix, 24
Prelutsky, Jack, 57, 167, 170, 173

Reeves, James, 84, 102
Resnikoff, Alexander, 89
Reznikoff, Charles, 187
Richards, Laura E., 67, 102
Ridlon, Marci, 56, 146
Roberts, Elizabeth Madox, 73
Ross, Abram Bunn, 53
Rossetti, Christina Georgina, 25, 39, 150, 151

Serraillier, Ian, 73, 100
Shakespeare, William, 158
Silverstein, Shel, 60, 108, 114
Stafford, William, 211
Stevenson, Robert Louis, 29, 83, 125, 127, 128, 129, 130
Swenson, May, 191, 196

Taylor, Jane, 32
Tennyson, Alfred, Lord, 77
Thackeray, William Makepeace, 64

Turner, Nancy Byrd, 54

Watson, Clyde, 19, 36, 44, 160
Whitman, Ruth, 206
Widerberg, Siv, 199, 200, 212
Willson, Dixie, 94
Wordsworth, William, 143
Worth, Valerie, 78, 86, 165, 189, 204
Wright, E. V. 48

Zolotow, Charlotte, 210